MW00768314

ISBN# 1-879239-07-8
1-3/96

Our sincere thanks to all the restaurant owners, operators and managers who contributed their valuable ideas to this book.

Graphics and design by Deborah Henckel and Teri Merbach.

Pour It On

52 Ways To Maximize Your Bar Profits

By Andrea Stewart

CONTENTS

CHAPTER ONE • The Manager 5

Introduction 5
Hiring and managing bartenders 6
Maximizing profits on your draft beer system 8
Ordering and managing your inventory 10
Negotiating with suppliers 12
Receiving expensive liquor shipments 14
Pricing beverage items 16
Controlling costs on all those "extras" 18
Cutting glassware costs 20
Garnishing drinks 22
Low-alcohol/non-alcohol drinks 24
Ice and ice machines 26
Increasing beverage sales starts with employee training 28
Conducting effective pre-shift team meetings 30
The art of effective role-playing 32
Teach servers and bartenders to sell 34
Implementing effective sales contests and incentives 36
Daily contests, daily rewards 38

CHAPTER TWO • The Staff 41

Using effective icebreakers and getting to know guests 42
Teaching product knowledge 44
Painting pictures with words and phrases 46
Positive body language helps increase sales 48
Train servers and bartenders to use sales props 50
Sales techniques to move everything on the menu 52
Upselling beer 54
The secrets of a "beer-clean" glass 56

Don't let your staff pour away your beer profits 58
Product knowledge is the key to selling hand-crafted beers 60
Recommending wines by the bottle 62
Training servers to sell and upsell wine 64
Training servers to open and pour wine 66
Wine pronunciation guide 68
Selling specialty drinks 70
Tips on selling and serving champagne 72
Selling after dinner drinks 74
Responsible alcohol service and ID checking 76

CHAPTER THREE • The Customer 79

Create an atmosphere where guests want to come back 80
Creating a marketing plan 82
Designing effective marketing materials 84
Stealing marketing/promotion ideas from the competition 86
Staffing up your marketing efforts 88
Get your suppliers involved in your marketing 90
Coordinate your marketing materials 92
Promotions for every occasion of the year 94
Presenting a profitable happy hour 96
Games and other activities to keep customers at the bar 98
Frequency clubs 100
Presenting beverage-related special events 102
Controlling marketing mailing costs 104
Satellite bars eliminate long lines at the bar 106
Maximizing summer bar profits by prepping your patio 108
Creating a wine list that encourages sales 110
Responsible drinking programs 112

READ THIS FIRST

Welcome to the age of step aerobics and bottled water. Whether it's a new American health consciousness or stricter drunk-driving legislation, people just don't *drink* like they used to. And while customers get more kicks from cappuccino, you're swallowing ever-increasing liquor prices. As new operations continue to pop up overnight, you find yourself doing battle with more competitors for fewer drinking customers. Kind of makes you want to convert to a health-food joint, doesn't it?

"You mix two jiggers of scotch to one jigger of Slim Fast. So far I've lost five pounds and my driver's license."
— Rocky Bridges on his diet

But it's not quite a return to Prohibition yet. Even with rising prices, liquor still provides the highest margin of anything on your menu. The more you serve, the better your bulk discounts — and the better your bar profits.

The first step toward maximizing those profits is to think of the bar business as a game of pennies. After all, your profit on beverage items never amounts to much more than a dollar. And you lose pennies off each dollar every time there's waste behind the bar, your server forgets to upsell to premium brands or your marketing efforts fail to bring traffic through your doors. To add to your bar profits, three things need to happen:

1. You have to get a handle on your bar's business. That means improving the way you manage your inventory, your equipment overhead, your supplier relationships and your bar staff.

2. Your staff has to have an intimate knowledge of your beverage products and the techniques necessary to sell them.

3. Your customers have to be enticed by your marketing efforts to come into your operation, spend more money on alcohol beverages and come back again — with their friends.

Read on for 52 ideas that will help you *Pour It On*, turning those pennies into dollars and adding profit to your bottom line.

HOW TO USE THIS BOOK

We've broken the book down into three chapters:

"The Manager" will show you how to better manage your bar's inventory, your supplier relationships, your equipment overhead and your bar and service staff.

"The Staff" will share training techniques on product knowledge, customer service, upselling and responsible alcohol service.

"The Customer" will let you in on effective marketing techniques to help you get more traffic through your doors and maximize your profit potential in the process.

Each of the 52 ideas is presented alongside a variety of related tips, techniques, samples, lists and philosophies, inspirational quotes and incentive ideas. We've designed the book this way so it's easy to read and absorb one idea at a time – one a week for a year, if you prefer, or a few ideas each day.

The wealth of ideas in this book apply to all types of operations – from fine-dining and casual-theme restaurants to pizza joints and neighborhood pubs. Granted, what works for your place may not work for the one down the street. Take the ideas you like, and leave those not to your taste here in the book.

Once you've finished reading the book, you can put these ideas to work for you by turning to the Action Plan in the back (page 114) and the subsequent "Bar Management," "Staff Training" and "Marketing" Strategies (pages 115-117).

**"Rule #1:
Don't sweat
the small stuff.
Rule #2:
When managed
well, it's all
small stuff."**

***— Jan Whitmire,
Director of Corporate
Development, Brinker
International***

CHAPTER ONE: THE MANAGER

Introduction

What's the secret to maximizing your bar profits? Details, details, details. As much as you're tempted to pass the buck, it's up to you to make sure all those details fall into place and that every penny counts.

The more pennies you make on every drink, the more dollars flow down the drain somewhere else. Even if you could control your liquor inventory and make sure that not a single drop is overpoured, there are a hundred other costly variables to deflate your bar's profits. Broken glassware, a foaming beer keg line, spoiled fruit garnishes, ice machine maintenance – the list goes on and on.

On the following pages are 17 ideas that can energize your bar's business. You'll learn how to negotiate with your suppliers for the best deals, how to make sure what arrives is exactly what you ordered, how to control costs on all those "extras" like napkins and swizzle sticks, and how to effectively train your bartenders and drink servers to maximize profits.

The Gold Standard

Hiring and managing bartenders

"What's the difference between a bartender and God? God doesn't think he's a bartender."
— Anonymous

Good bartenders are worth their weight in gold – literally. If drinks are measured accurately, taste "just right" and are served quickly and efficiently, you can count on a profitable business.

Too often, though, you'll find bartenders who are "in business" for themselves, pocketing a few dollars here and there, overpouring to their big tippers and giving away a few to their friends.

To find a good bartender, look for honesty, personality and mechanics first. The candidate who has memorized and can prepare the greatest variety of cocktails may not be the best candidate for the job. Better to have a drink recipe book handy than to hire a mix-master who pockets more than he sells.

One way to guard against bartenders who give freebies is to delegate a manager to back-up bar service, especially during busy shifts. The management presence will not only keep the bartender honest, but also provide extra help when the bar gets hopping. Teach that manager to pay close attention. Figure out what the regulars drink and who the bartender's friends are.

Conduct regular audits of the bar's cash drawer – at least once a week – to reveal any thievery. If the till should come out over what receipts indicate, you have a bartender in need of additional training in cash handling.

Most often, though, you'll find only minor discrepancies. For instance, if the cash register says you've sold 22 shots of Jagermeister but there's a whole bottle missing, you may have a bartender with a heavy hand. Too free a free pour can spell trouble for your bottom line.

What does that extra splash really cost? Probably not a whole lot if it's just one drink, but 200 overpoured drinks a shift at a conservative 10 cents a splash adds up to $20 per shift, $40 per day – $14,560 per year!

The solution? Never, ever allow free pouring. Utilize pre-measured automatic dispensing systems and jiggers instead. Buy good quality shot glasses with pour lines marked on them. And monitor the bartender as much as possible.

Measure for Measure

Some advocates of free-pouring say that using a jigger in front of the customer sends a negative message about your operation's frugality. But as one manager says, "Yeah, every bartender I've ever had to fire has used that as an excuse." The days of the four-finger highball are gone – and the public knows that. Bartenders can still use a jigger with flair and the guest won't think twice about it. Besides, the minute you start giving things away is the minute your business begins to fail. There are other perks a bartender can provide guests – value for their money, entertainment and a fun experience, to name a few.

Draft Dodging

Maximizing profits on your draft beer system

"Business is more than making money. Losing less money is sometimes important, too."
— *Kim Woo-Choong, Every Street Is Paved with Gold*

Consumers perceive draft beer to be of higher quality than bottled beer. For the most part, that's true. But draft beer, so sensitive to its environment and the equipment that brings it to the tap, requires special handling and care. Sometimes maintaining a healthy and profitable draft beer dispensing system can be a costly headache.

But that's not to say you should shut down your kegs. Your margins on draft beers are typically a bit higher than on bottled varieties, so it makes good sense to offer them. That's why you should heed the following tips to help you maximize your draft beer profits while providing your customers with the freshest, tastiest brews available.

- Invest in "Empty Beer Detector" valves for all your keg lines. Typically when a keg empties, you lose about five pitchers of beer as the line fills with foam. At $3.25 a glass, five glasses per pitcher, that's a loss of about $80 for *each* empty keg. "EBD" valves automatically shut off the keg, holding all but 8-12 inches of beer in the line without causing the usual foaming. When you re-tap, only that foot needs to be refilled, wasting just 2-4 ounces. At a cost of around $85, EBD valves pay for themselves in just one or two kegs.

- Beer is highly sensitive to both temperature and pressure, and foams as a result. If the beer is allowed to warm, liquid and gas separate and gas bubbles form in the lines, sending foam and profits down the drain. Keep your cooler between 36 to 38 degrees and maintain the temperature by limiting staff trips into the walk-in.

- And look into a cooling apparatus for the beer lines themselves. One operator pumps an antifreeze/water mixture (chilled to 30 degrees) through copper coolant lines affixed along each beer line. Foam insulation is then wrapped around the outside to contain the cool temperatures.
- Keep a careful eye on the system's pressure. Without enough pressure, beer will flow too slowly and tend to go flat. Too much pressure causes beer to overcarbonate. The ideal dispensing pressure range is between 14 p.s.i. and 18 p.s.i. Be sure your secondary pressure regulators are set for each line, since internal keg pressure varies with the type of beer, the length of keg line and the direction it flows.

Chem 101

The usual CO_2/compressed air dispensing system can cause draft problems, too. Trace elements and odors – smoke from the bar, kitchen odors, leaked oil from the compressor, etc. – in compressed air can affect the beer's taste. And the pure oxygen causes beer to lose carbonation more quickly. Check into a CO_2/nitrogen mixture as an alternative. Beer needs CO_2 to maintain its natural carbonation. But if it sits too long or the line's pressure setting is too high, the beer will overcarbonate. Nitrogen in the mix helps to "dilute" it. A CO_2/nitrogen combination may cost a little more, but it's worth it. In some markets you can buy the gases pre-blended or save a bit by blending them on-site with two tanks and a $125 "blender."

3 A Place For Everything

Ordering and managing your inventory

Storage space is a hot commodity in most operations — especially when it comes to all the products you need behind your bar. Beer and white wine take up precious refrigerated space. Your draft beer system requires its own refrigerated room. And spirits and bottled beers that don't have to be refrigerated should be stored in a locked room since liquor is a big attraction for light fingers.

"You can have the best product in the world. But if you can't sell it, you've still got it."
— Diamond Jim Brady

There are so many liquor, beer and wine brands in the world today that no bar can hope to stock them all. Nor would bar managers or owners wishing to preserve their sanity seek to do so. The larger the inventory, the more work is generated and the more space is required. For maximum efficiency and profit, keep your inventory lean and mean.

Think of your inventory as an investment you're not getting a return on. Pay careful attention to every deal your vendors offer. Too often they aren't deals at all. You lose money every day your over-ordered merchandise sits around. Say, for example, you went ahead with a 10-case deal on schnapps. You ran some specials but it turns out that brand has lost its popularity. As it sits in your storeroom, another supplier offers you a deal on vodka. You know your servers can move the extra vodka, but you don't have room to store it because of all that schnapps. Unless you can find space elsewhere you'll have to pass up the vodka deal.

Plus, extra inventory is more susceptible to theft and careless waste. If there are two cases of Grand Marnier sitting around, it's easier for someone to steal a bottle without being noticed. But if there were just two bottles, maybe the potential culprit would think twice.

That's why you should look for ways to economize your inventory. For instance, some operators can get away with carrying only one brand of beer. They're usually fine-dining establishments that do a lot more volume in bottled wine. Maybe there's something on your menu you could sacrifice. The key is to know your customer base.

And know your inventory at all times. Ordering isn't something you should do once a week. Sure, you'll probably only place one order a week, but look through your product every day. Talk to your bartenders about what's selling. Know what your regulars drink. Say you have a customer who drinks a lot of B&B. If he's going out of town for a month you can cut back your order. Keep careful records of how your product needs change with the seasons – more tequila in the summer, more brandies in the winter.

Stay in the Loop

Sure, you should talk to your bartenders about which liquor items are selling and which aren't, but many operations make the mistake of delegating all the ordering and inventory of bar items to their key bartender. It may not be such a good idea. While it may save a busy manager valuable time, elevating a bartender into a pseudo management position can be less cost-efficient and more of a headache. Bartenders may know their products, but they often don't have a clear vision of your operation's profit and loss quotient. A deal that sounds good to the bartender may not be all that great overall. Plus, it pulls the manager out of the loop, which is exactly where he or she needs to be to oversee ordering and inventory most effectively.

The Art of the Deal

Negotiating with suppliers

"The will to win is not as important as the will to prepare to win."
— Bobby Knight

There's a fine line between negotiating and haggling over deals with your suppliers. Just where do you draw the line between being "savvy" and "downright unreasonable?"

Of course you want to maximize concessions received and minimize concessions given. But remember that your supplier wants the same. You both want to win. The only people who should be "winning" are your customers. Even if you succeed in obtaining a good discount, the prices will surely be made up elsewhere.

Generally prices for beer, wine and liquor are set across the board. But even though negotiating price isn't usually an option, you may be able to negotiate other terms of the deal: point-of-sale marketing materials, frequency of deliveries – even on-site waitstaff sales training to help move more of a particular supplier's product.

Let your suppliers know that their prices and services will be continually monitored and compared with the competition. A savvy operator will add new suppliers to his or her approved supplier list and drop those who don't perform to high standards. This practice is not followed "on whim," but rather to show suppliers that those who do a good job will have your business. Those who don't – won't.

It's easy to get caught up in their promotions. But, remember, that promotional deal has to be satisfying to both you and the supplier. When you allow a supplier or manufacturer to come in and present a promotion, you're subjecting your greatest asset – your customer base – to the whims of someone outside your operation. Don't let them call all the shots.

Look for the kind of promotions that will generate more business for your operation. Insist that your suppliers not only supply product, but training materials so your waitstaff is familiarized with the product – and more important, the product category – well before they begin pushing it on your guests.

And be sure they supply their own staffers for the promotion. Your managers shouldn't have to let other management functions fall by the wayside as they scurry about trying to present your suppliers' promotions.

Playing the Game

Manufacturers know the game: The only way they'll ever get your bar to carry their unique new beverage item is by creating such a huge customer demand through expensive advertising that you'll find yourself losing business if you don't carry the item. But you don't have to spend a lifetime in the business to see a few brands come and go. It's estimated that just one in 20 new beverage products "catches on" with the mass market and becomes a standard bar item. So beware the "Trojan Horse" method of product introduction many manufacturers employ – and don't buy heavily into a product just because the manufacturer has invented and advertised a chic-sounding cocktail that just happens to have its product as an essential ingredient. When that advertising stops, usually the hype will, too, and the item will sit on a dusty corner of your bar until it gets thrown out.

5 Liquid Gold

Receiving expensive liquor shipments

To be on the receiving end of a liquor shipment is like receiving goods for Fort Knox. Think of your beverage storeroom as a bank vault — full of liquid gold.

And because liquor is such an expensive item to have on stock, it's a good idea to have three people receiving the goods. Why? Because it's physically easier for two people to do receiving and physical inventory.

The third person, ideally, is you or the person who placed the order in the first place. And the best tool for the third person is not a hand truck, but a calculator — used to double-check the shipment against the invoice to be sure what was received is, in fact, just what was ordered.

Simply counting the number of cases received isn't enough. Open the cases and carefully review the contents — especially if you've ordered wines of specific vintages.

You should double-check the math on the invoice, as well. It's not that your vendors aren't to be trusted. You wouldn't be working with them if you didn't trust them, right? But they are human, and everyone makes mistakes. One little extra zero on any of the figures can cost you a mint.

Careful, also, of those vendors who ship more products than you originally ordered to add to their sales quota for the week. They're counting on you to be the good Samaritan who'll say, "Well as long as it's here ...." Don't.

"The buck stops here."

— President Harry S. Truman

Send it back with the appropriate credit memo. Accepting more products than are actually desired can lead to excessive inventories and, usually, waste.

Stagger the delivery times of your different vendors. You don't need all those delivery people running into each other – and you. Plus, it will make your receiving duties less hectic if you're only checking one order at a time. Set regular delivery hours so that you'll always be present to stay on top of things.

Make sure your vendor contracts all include a clause that says you have the right to refuse items of poor quality or in poor condition and have replacements sent back at no delivery charge. You need to ask for this service up front so that you know that the items you need will be there when you need them.

It Happens

Do you have a back-up plan for those not-so-rare occasions when you run out of a liquor item days before your scheduled delivery? Nothing wastes more money than asking your vendor to deliver more product earlier than what was scheduled. Not only will you incur a bundle in additional delivery charges, you may end up overstocking the item when that original delivery finally arrives. Careful ordering will usually prevent this fiasco. But sometimes it can't be helped. Watch the paper for local liquor store deals close to your vendor discounts. The deals will never be as good, but weigh the extra price against your vendor's extra delivery charges – you may come out ahead. Before you head to the liquor store, though, check your local laws. It's illegal in some states for operators to buy retail. Other states limit the amount of liquor you can purchase at retail outlets per year.

6 How Much?

Pricing beverage items

The fine art of pricing your drink items can be easier than dealing with food for the simple reason that spirits, wine and beer can be easier to order, receive, store and handle.

Plus, pricing is often set by your competition since prices are pretty standard in the industry. If your drinks are priced inconsistently with the bar next door, your customers will certainly take notice.

But you can't operate with prices too low for your overhead. Look through your menu prices at least once a year to evaluate if you're on target.

All things being perfect, with no "evaporation" due to theft or waste, pricing your beverage items begins with knowing exactly what each of your drinks costs per ounce. Because alcohol beverage bottles are in metric sizes, be careful that you first convert metric equivalents to ounces and then price by the ounce.

On an ounce-by-ounce basis, comparison is easier between brands and different container sizes. Usually the larger the container, the lower the cost per ounce. But on the other hand, you'll need to consider whether that larger container is too large to easily handle, resulting in wasteful spillage.

The way you handle your prime alcohol costs can significantly decrease your bottom line if not carefully handled. Every percentage point between product cost and percentages of your cost standard is important.

"Value is not low pricing. It is a quality product at a fair price combined with excellent service."

— Stan Novack, VP Beverage Products & Concepts, Host Marriott

For example, you've already figured out that 22 percent is your cost standard, or what you need to reach your desired profit line. Look at your invoices and you may find that your actual cost on liquor was $600,000 or 22.7 percent, just .7 percent above your cost standard. "Great," you say, "Not even three-quarters of a percentage point." You may think you're on target, but your operation is actually taking a big hit. Take that .7 percent and convert it to a dollar figure: .007 x $600,000 = $4,200 more to produce the same $600,000 worth of revenue.

You could have purchased 50 cases of scotch or vodka, which in turn could have produced an additional $19,090.91 in sales. The higher your sales volume, the more each percentage point is worth and the more important it is for you to watch this line item.

Appearance Is Everything

While you may not be able to out-price the operation next door, you may be able to out-*present* them. All it takes is a little creativity. Have your bartender play around with some more popular drink recipes to come up with "drama drinks" — unique combinations of low-cost mixers, fruit and garnishes served in big, unique glassware. You'll be able to charge a little more, but keep costs about the same. When customers notice the exciting specialty drinks your servers parade around the room, they'll want a few on their table.

Extra, Extra

Controlling costs on all those "extras"

Even if you're able to get a handle on all your alcohol costs, your operation's profitability can still go down the tubes if you can't control costs on all those "extras" that every bar has to have: napkins, ashtrays, straws, swizzle sticks.

"Any day you don't learn something new, you're just not paying attention."

— Mike Plunkett, Regional Manager, Dave & Buster's

Piece by piece, none of these items costs all that much. But multiply those costs by your rate of consumption and you'll quickly see where all your profits are going. Consider the following cost-effective options:

- What's the easiest way to double your specialty drink sales this year? Use bigger straws. It's a principle so deceptively simple that it slips by many operators. If you use the typical tiny swizzle straws, your guests will sip slowly. But switch to the same size straws a fast-food joint would put in a chocolate shake, and your guests will gulp. They'll go through their drink twice as fast and order another. It's particularly effective in your jumbo frozen drinks — daiquiris, margaritas, etc. No one likes a straw that clogs up. For just pennies more, you'll provide a service to your guests that also increases your overall sales. What more could you want?
- While you're at it, replace those disposable swizzle straws with real glass or durable plastic swizzle sticks. They're easy to wash and more economical in the long run because they're reusable.
- Use coasters instead of napkins. People don't save those napkins imprinted with your operation's logo as much as

you think they do. Who wants a soggy wad of paper as a souvenir, anyway? Besides, every time there's a spill, your bartender wastes about 50 of those dinky napkins to blot it up. Keep a few extra towels behind the bar, instead. And have coasters imprinted with your operation's logo. Maybe a few ash trays, too. You'll be able to reuse them for years – and they'll make much better souvenirs for your customers.

- You'll save even more if you use the logoed coasters and ash trays provided by your manufacturers. Beer, wine and liquor companies often provide these at no cost, while they may charge you for logoed napkins.
- For *real* savings, talk to the only manufacturers out there today who are often willing to provide anything for free – cigarette companies who have found that logoed merchandise is one of the few sources of advertising they're still legally allowed.

Mixing It Up

Do you and your bartenders know when it's best to use an upright electric mixer or when it's time to break out the blender? As a rule of thumb, an upright electric mixer is ideal for quickly mixing drinks with sweet and sour, juices and/or cream, such as a margarita or a planter's punch. You should only need to break out the blender for frozen specialty drinks or drinks that require blending in fresh fruits. It's valuable information for everyone, since using that blender takes extra prep and clean-up time for the bartender. If your operation sells a lot of blended drinks, consider installing a frozen drink dispensing machine that will keep those summer favorites ready to serve.

8 Glass Houses

Cutting glassware costs

"Fortune is like glass — the brighter the glitter, the more easily broken."
— Publius, First Century, BC

When the bar gets hopping during a Friday happy hour, who's the only person in the room who doesn't cheer at the sound of a glass shattering as it hits the floor? It's the sound that makes every bar or restaurant manager cringe.

What's frustrating is that the most breakable item in your bar or restaurant is the one item you have to provide for every single guest. Here are some suggestions for getting a handle on your glassware replacement costs:

- Always hand-wash stemware and other fragile glassware at the bar. This keeps them out of the dish room where most breakage occurs.
- The fewer types of glasses you have the easier your life will be. The more varieties you use the more time you spend on inventory and ordering. Most bars can work efficiently with just six or seven types of glasses. Who says you have to serve champagne in tulip flutes? Order a few more wine glasses and no one will complain.
- Be creative in putting drinks into different-size glasses to maximize the use of one variety – and take advantage of bulk buys. Guests usually won't mind, unless the different size provides less drink for the same money.
- Before you purchase, select a few samples and run them through a "fitness test" to see how they stand up to hand and machine washing. Put each one through the same rigors it would be subjected to on a busy night.

- Consider serving beverages in non-traditional glasses or even plain mugs. Many operations find that mason jars fit nicely into their theme. They buy just two sizes of jars – cheaper than regular glassware anyway – in mass quantities and serve everything in them. Use your imagination. Are there similar alternatives that will work for your concept?
- Some operations have found that offering specialty glassware as a giveaway not only reduces their breakage costs, but can be a profitable promotion that attracts people through the front doors. Just combine unique glassware with a tasty drink at a good price and you've got yourself a "keep the glass" promotion. People love to collect unusual glasses. Customers often collect entire table settings of popular margarita, martini or hurricane glasses.

Glassware Handling

Share the following do's and don'ts of glassware management with your staff to cut down your breakage costs:

Don't:

Let the beer tap bang against the rim of a glass.

Store silverware in glasses.

Put cold glasses into a warm dishwasher or put cold liquids into a warm or hot glass.

Use a glass for an ice scoop.

Pick up glasses in bouquets.

Do:

Dump ice out of glasses.

Sort items in bus trays.

Check glassware storage. Are your breakables kept in a handy place or do bartenders break glasses just getting them off the shelf?

Double check staffing. Do you have enough bartenders on?

All Dressed Up

Garnishing drinks

When it comes to garnishing specialty drinks, we've come a long way from those tiny umbrellas and maraschino cherries. The better the garnish, the more eye appeal you'll create and the more drinks you'll sell. When customers see festive-looking drinks paraded through the dining room, they'll want to order a few for their table.

"Happiness is a hungry man finding two olives in his martini."
—Johnny Carson

That's why you should strive to be creative, even wacky, with your beverage garnishes. Here are a few ideas to get your creative juices flowing:

- Hollow licorice sticks for straws
- Dry ice to make drinks bubble and "smoke"
- "Shishkabobs" of fruit
- Huge strawberries, plain or dipped in sugar
- Fruit and spice-flavored candy canes
- Star fruit, mango or kiwi slices
- Black and green olives stuffed with almonds
- Shrimp, string beans, asparagus, jalapeños or red and white onion wedges for Bloody Mary's
- Sparklers "grounded" by fruit pieces
- Colorful, loopy straws

But don't let drink garnishes swallow your profits. If dressing up drinks with "extras" doesn't help generate sales, stop spending money on them!

And when the traditional fruit items you use for garnishes go out of season, look for alternatives. Fruit can be a huge expense if you feel trapped into spending off-season prices. Consider offering those drinks only during season.

Be careful not to cut up too much fruit. Instead of having the daytime bartender cut fruit for both the day and night shifts, schedule the second-shift bartender to come in a few minutes early to prepare the fruit he'll need for his own shift. If he runs out, he'll need to cut some more. Not only will there be fewer shriveled up leftovers for tomorrow's shift, you'll lay more of the responsibility on the bartender – so there should be less fruit wasted.

Fruits of Thy Labors

Want to keep your fruit garnishes fresher longer? Follow these tips:

- **Thoroughly wash fruit trays and troughs every day.**
- **Use a cutting board and a clean knife to cut fruits – never the bar top.**
- **To extract more juice from citrus fruits, warm the fruit under running water.**
- **To keep lime wedges and lemon twists fresher longer, store them in their trays on top of a napkin saturated with club soda.**
- **Cover freshly cut fruits to protect from dust, oxidation and insects.**
- **Cover and store cherries, olives and onions in their own juices to retain freshness and visual appeal.**

10 On the Wagon

Low-alcohol/non-alcohol drinks

> **"I feel sorry for anyone who doesn't drink. Every morning when they wake up they know that's the best they're gonna feel all day."**
> ***— Robert Mitchum***

Is your operation attracting more non-drinkers these days? There's still plenty of profit to be made. Just be sure your operation offers what they want. Creative non-alcohol or low-alcohol specialty drinks, for example, can be a big draw with today's more responsible drinking crowd – and can provide a healthy profit for your operation.

Take a look through all the ingredients kept behind the bar. Nearly a quarter contain little or no alcohol – juices, mixers, fresh fruits, etc. That means endless opportunity for a creative bartender who can mix up a dazzling array of "mocktails." Think of it this way – all those items are required for other drinks, so you have to stock them. Selling more non-alcohol drinks reduces waste and leads to savings from bulk discounts.

Non-alcohol beers and wines have come a long way, too. So consider keeping a small inventory for those who request them. Lunchtime, for example, is a prime opportunity to suggest non-alcohol brews. Train servers the right dialogue to use if a guest declines their beer suggestion because they have to "go back to work": "*Today we're featuring O'Doul's. It's a non-alcohol brew from Anheuser-Busch that tastes great and won't slow you down this afternoon*."

And although no ethical establishment would (or could, for long) deceive customers by serving alcohol substitutes disguised as the real things, many are serving "lightened" versions of standard drinks, especially those that call for more than one type of liquor. Try using non-alcohol triple sec in your Long Island Iced Tea recipe, for example. With vodka, gin and rum already mixed in, it will taste the same as traditional recipes but contain slightly less alcohol. It costs much less to make since premium triple sec typically ranges from $7 and $12.50 per 750 ml, while comparable non-alcohol brands cost between $3 and $5.50. The savings add up even more if you use it in all your cocktails that require triple sec: kamikazes, margaritas, daiquiris, mai tais. Most margarita drinkers want their alcohol to come from a good tequila – not triple sec. And you can pass the savings on to the customer by lowering drink prices. Look, also, for opportunities to use non- or low-alcohol peach schnapps, blue Curaçao, creme de banana, creme de coco or creme de menthe.

And since operators are often held responsible for alcohol-related accidents, you can lower your liability by training bartenders the right dialogue for selling reduced-alcohol and non-alcohol beverages. For instance: *"Are you driving? How about I make you a special non-alcohol version of that drink?"*

Water, Water Everywhere

There's no such thing as a "free" glass of water. In fact, it can cost up to $1.08. Share these points with your servers and bartenders to show why they should suggest non-alcohol specialty drinks and beers when non-drinking customers request "just water." That glass has to be ordered, inventoried, filled and washed for each guest – up go labor costs. When one breaks, it must be replaced. The cost of soap, dishwasher rental or depreciation, heat, gas and water – hot to clean the glass and cold to fill it – all add to the cost, too. The ice-cube machine runs all day and the air around it must be ventilated – up go the water and electric bills. But the fact that will really get their attention is this: Which is better – 15 percent of $3 or 15 percent of nothing?

Cool Runnings

Ice and ice machines

Ever have one of those days? It's 98 degrees outside, the patio's packed with festive margarita drinkers and the ice machine, leaking rivers across the floor, is doing its best impression of whale mating calls. Oh, to be in Europe where most everything is served at room temperature. Ice may be nothing more than *really cold* water, but it's one ingredient no bar or restaurant can do without.

"I always wake up at the crack of ice."
— *Joe E. Louis*

Unfortunately, most operators don't spend a lot of time thinking about their ice machines until something goes wrong. And something always goes wrong. Think about it – your ice machine runs all the time. That's why its most important feature is a good warranty and service contract. Most carry three-year parts and labor, but look for better – and watch out for those that cover just one year. Here are a few other aspects of ice machines you should consider:

- Since your ice needs will change with the seasons, decide on the capacity you need during your busiest months – usually during the summer. Some operations find that their needs drop to about half the usual consumption during the winter.

- So rather than running one enormous machine all year round, keep two smaller machines going through the summer, and shut one down during winter months to save on electricity costs.

- Location is everything. Most operators find that the only available space big enough is in their kitchen. But placing an air-cooled machine that shoots out hot air into an already-hot kitchen will cause your air conditioning costs to skyrocket. Either look into a water-cooled system or find a new location altogether. Keep in mind that a water-cooled system can be less efficient in the summertime when you need it most.

- And regardless of the cooling system, proper ventilation is required. Perhaps there's a better location elsewhere in the restaurant? Since space is at a premium in most operations, ice machine companies are beginning to experiment with different shapes and sizes. Some operators may find that a compact under-bar unit or vertical setup works better for their limited space.

Not Now!

There's nothing worse than running out of ice when you need it most. That's why you should design a system for managing your ice supply during your peak seasons. For instance, during the busy summer "margarita" months, bag up ice as quickly as your ice machine produces it and stack the extra bags in your freezer. That way, your ice machine is never full so it works at its highest capacity – and you have a surplus of ice on hand when you need it.

No Train, No Gain

Increasing beverage sales starts with employee training

"The more you expect from people, the more you have to train them."
— Geoff Bailey, Colorado Restaurateur

The road to increasing beverage revenues begins in the training room. You can do everything else right – marketing, purchasing and cost-cutting – but it's those front-of-the-house employees, your servers and bartenders, who decide whether you're able to keep customers coming through the door and move the merchandise you've purchased.

Your employees are the last and most important link in the chain between you and the customer. That's why you have to show them how to do things right.

Well-trained employees will not only help you increase sales of everything on your menu, they'll help you acquire and maintain more customers by providing better service.

Recognize them by training and re-training them monthly, daily – even hourly, customizing your approach to suit every server and bartender. Make it your personal goal to teach everyone on your staff something new every day.

Effective training begins with preparation. Decide what your sales and service goals are, then use your training sessions to communicate those goals to everyone on your staff.

Base your training on the behavior you expect and not just attitude. You can have the best attitude in the world, but if your behavior doesn't change, there's no improvement.

"But training time is money," say most operators who complain that they have no time for regular training. Consider the costs of subjecting your guests to an untrained staff.

What if bad service drives just one customer away? The dollar cost of losing just one guest may not seem like much, but what if that guest convinces friends and family about the bad experience. You'll lose potential guests who've never even been to your place.

Consider the alternative: What if your well-trained staff provides such *good* service, that same guest comes in once a week instead of once a month, bringing friends and family along? What if your well-trained server convinces this guest to always order a premium liquor in his cocktails and order an appetizer? Effective staff training will make you or break you.

Keep It Fun

Don't use what little training time you have to drone on about dress codes, policies and procedures. That's why most managers and staffers hate training and why most sessions fail to communicate any valuable skills employees can use on the floor. Nothing lasts as long as a box of cereal you don't like and a training session you can't stand. Make your training fun, lively and relevant. Appeal to all the senses by using fun visual aids like flip charts and colorful markers, props, videos and workbooks, flash cards and little tokens, like lotto tickets or dollar bills, to reward participation. Use role-play sessions to help test the newly learned skills and follow up on the floor, providing constant feedback as employees develop their skills.

13 Shift Into Gear

Conducting effective pre-shift team meetings

"Is management's unwillingness to train daily caused by ignorance or apathy? I don't know and I don't care."
— Anonymous

Daily training? Most managers respond to that call with a hearty, "Yeah ... fat chance." It's not like you don't have enough to do already, right? But if maximizing bar sales is your priority, you'll need your front-of-the-house staff to help you do it.

The only way to achieve *your* bar sales goals is to teach your bartenders and servers techniques they can use to improve their service and increase their sales. And the best way to do that is to train, test, retrain and re-test those skills *every day*.

Training daily may not be as difficult as you fear — not if you hold brief team meetings before each shift. Here are some tips on managing them effectively:

- Keep the meeting short and sweet, five or 10 minutes per day. Always start and end the meetings on time.
- Keep distractions to a minimum. Don't hold the meeting facing windows or in high-traffic areas. It's hard enough to keep the attention of the short-attention-span crowd. Don't compound your problems by creating distractions that could have easily been avoided.
- Think dialogue, not monologue. Managers should speak 20 percent of the time and seek feedback during the other 80 percent. The best way to do that is to involve participants in the discussion. For example, instead of *you* telling staffers how to upsell cocktail

orders, call on your top servers and bartenders to describe the techniques that have made *them* successful. Encourage feedback.

- Conduct brief role-playing scenarios during which servers and bartenders can practice their new techniques.
- Use the fear of being called upon to keep them focused. Verbally quiz employees on product knowledge, daily specials and upcoming events or promotions.
- Encourage employees to practice the new skills during the next shift. Set daily sales and service goals and introduce incentives.
- Use this time to recognize good performances from the previous shift. Conclude by commending individual sales and service efforts from the previous 24 hours.
- Follow up during the next shift to be sure staff members have retained what you've taught them.

Personal Time

If your operation staggers employees' shifts, you can still conduct effective pre-shift meetings – they'll just be shorter and more individualized. Make it a rule for staffers to seek out a trainer for a five-minute personal training session before they go out on the floor. Have a regular meeting place where you hang a flip chart with that day's training focus written on it, as well as a daily incentive overview and the names of the previous day's incentive winners. The trainer should first do a uniform review, then spend two minutes going over current promotions and specials. A brief product knowledge quiz should come next, then the trainer should work with the employee to set a sales goal for the day.

14 Show Me the Way

The art of effective role-playing

> **"It takes just as much time to show employees how to do it right as it would to tell them they did it wrong."**
> ***— Steve Sa, Area Manager, Double Eagle Distributors, Deerfield Beach, Fla.***

As the old Chinese proverb goes: "I hear and I forget, I see and I remember, I do and I understand." Sure, training your servers and bartenders effective sales and service behaviors will help you increase your bar sales, but to really make the most of your training, you need to put those employees "in the driver's seat" where they can try out their new behaviors and skills.

Add role-playing sessions to every pre-shift, monthly or quarterly meeting. This effective training technique will help you reinforce your staff training on everything from suggestive selling and learning guests' names to product knowledge and smiling, friendly service.

More important, by letting your servers and bartenders role-play their new skills and behaviors on "play-actor customers," you can evaluate their mastery of those skills *before* you set them loose on your *real* customers.

Still, many managers believe all they need to do at training sessions is be a good speaker and scribble on a flip chart.

Sure, that's all part of it. But think back to how you learned to drive and you'll see why role-playing is so important. Did you have someone explain it on a flip chart then jump into a $50,000 hot rod? Probably not.

Most of us had someone *show* us the proper techniques. Then we practiced over and over – on wet roads, on dry roads, in traffic, on open highways — until we felt confident enough with our skills to drive the DMV heavy around the block a few times. It wasn't until after *he* gave us the green light that someone handed us the keys.

Think of all the individual sections in your bar or restaurant as $50,000 hot rods since each of those sections is capable of generating at least that much in annual gross sales. And don't hand over the keys until you've tested your employees' sales and service skills through role-playing exercises.

Effective role-playing in five easy steps

- **Write scenarios on notecards in advance and write out customer dialogue on "cheat sheets."**
- **On a flip chart, write three specific behaviors, like upselling, learning guests' names and offering a choice.**
- **Call up role-players one scenario at a time. Don't just pick good servers or bad servers. Give everyone a chance.**
- **Afterward, critique by asking the audience "What, if anything, could have been done better?" Detail any missed opportunities.**
- **Review the main points and ask the group "What are you going to do differently as a result of today's training?"**

Think Sales

Teach servers and bartenders to sell

Train your servers and bartenders to think and act like salespeople. Why? As the legendary restaurateur Diamond Jim Brady once said, "You can have the best product in the world. But if you can't sell it, you've still got it."

"Everyone lives by selling something."
— Robert Louis Stevenson

You've got a wine cellar stacked to the brim and case upon case of spirits in the storage room. Teach your servers and bartenders just a few basic sales techniques and you'll watch those rooms empty in half the time — with twice the money in the cash drawer.

Plus, the more your staff can sell within the same time period, the better the bulk discounts you can get from your vendors, which increases your margins even more.

Besides, your servers will make a lot more money (as much as $2,500 a year or more!) which will make them happier employees — cutting down on turnover costs.

Perhaps most important, when servers make helpful suggestions, guests feel as if they've received better service. A server who makes suggestions is perceived to be more in tune to their needs. That will keep those guests coming back. Which makes your restaurant more profitable — which, in turn, will make you a happier manager, which will make you treat your employees better, which means happier employees who stay with the restaurant longer. Such is the cycle of success!

So where do you begin? Invest in sales training programs that will teach your employees the art of suggestive selling.

Tell your sales staff that all they have to do is learn more about the products on the menu and wine list and make a few recommendations – and the worst that will happen is the guest may say "No."

If your sales training encourages just one server to increase check averages $1 per guest –upgrading from well to premium liquor in a cocktail or selling a $16 bottle of wine to every fourth four-top – and that server waits on, say, 50 guests per shift, you'll have added another $30,000 to your bottom line this year. That's just one server. *Now* imagine what your whole waitstaff could do...

Work Smarter, Not Harder

Another plus to sales training is it teaches bartenders and servers to work smarter, not harder – which means less time in "The Weeds" where even adequate service is impossible. With sales training, you'll be able to turn your "order-takers" into "service-oriented salespeople" who are able to guide guests through the menu and drink lists, making suggestions and answering guests' questions. Servers will be able to control their sections, saving steps along the way, instead of letting their sections control them.

16 Eyes on the Prize

Implementing effective sales contests and incentives

"The point of contests, incentives and recognition programs is that they make everyone feel that service and sales are his or her individual responsibility. That not only leads to better service for the customer, it also means higher morale for the staff."

— Lauren O'Connell, Citicorp

You can rant and rave about increasing sales of beverage items, but it won't mean a lot to your employees who are just trying to get through their shift with a few bucks in their pocket. Maximizing bar sales is *your* goal. Not theirs.

You can, however, create a motivation for those employees to *help* you succeed. Incentives and contests are effective, low-cost techniques you can use to motivate employees to do just about anything: sales, service or cost cutting.

But don't start passing out hundred-dollar bills and microwaves just yet. There are some things you need to consider before you implement an employee incentive program:

- Start with the end in mind. Determine your specific desired result before you begin and incentive program. Then plan and set goals backward.
- Communicate that goal to your staff in terms they'll understand. If, for instance, you want to increase your bottled wine sales by 10 percent this month, don't tell them, "*To achieve this goal, we must sell 1,200 more bottles this month*." Break it down for them: "*If we just sell 40 more bottles of wine per day, 20 per shift — that's only two per server, per shift. We can easily achieve this goal*." It will inspire your staff to see how their individual efforts contribute to the big picture.
- Be sure to choose the type of contest or incentive that's most appropriate for the staffers involved. Con-

tests for servers and bartenders should be based on number of items sold during a particular promotion, percentage of check average increase, sales per hour, or gross sales per customer.

- Post a contest board so everyone can see their progress. Reward those who achieve goals and re-train those who don't.
- Structure your incentives and contests so there will be several winners. Reward not only the highest check averages or highest sales per hour, but also the most-improved sales percentage. It will eliminate the "same-server-always-wins" syndrome.
- Celebrate winners publicly. Award prizes at team meetings. Take Polaroid pictures of winners holding their prizes and hang the photos in the kitchen under the banner "This Month's Winners." Be enthusiastic when you make the presentations, and show the non-winners how to succeed in the next contest by analyzing the behavior of the current winners.

The Prize Is Right

Choose appropriate rewards. Many programs fail when the winner is given a prize that doesn't justify the effort. Ask employees what kind of prizes would motivate them to improve their sales and service performances. Award merchandise, not cash. Merchandise can't be spent, and it has "trophy" value. You want your staff members to see the results of their winning efforts every day. Be creative in selecting prizes: Awards can include watches, cameras, CDs or tapes – even a quick-pick Lotto ticket for their "million-dollar" effort. Another good prize is a gift certificate to another restaurant. It will provide the employee with a lasting memory for his or her winning efforts.

Instant Gratification

Daily contests, daily rewards

"Motivation is something you have to create each day. What you did yesterday doesn't count today."

— *Bill Flock, President of Bill Flock & Associates*

Sales contests are great tools for boosting morale, while encouraging servers to try out new sales techniques. Great salespeople are very competitive and they love contests because they like to win. But sometimes long sales contests get too tedious and servers give up half way through.

Research has shown that contests and incentives for hourly workers get the best results when held, measured and rewarded within a 28-day period. Employees tend to lose interest in a contest after a month, no matter how great the theme you've chosen or how well it's organized. So keep your contests short and simple.

Consider also setting up a new mini-contest every day. It will give servers something to look forward to on every shift, without the burnout of longer contests.

Prizes don't have to be as big as, say, a new car. They could be as simple as your operation's own "funny money" (play money employees can use for purchases at your restaurant). So the cost to the operation is negligible compared to the increase in check averages brought on by the servers' extra efforts.

Month-long contests are normally most effective for only nine days — the first four of the month and the last five. To keep your contest interesting and interactive, consider offering small, daily rewards to servers and bartenders who hit their daily goals, especially during the middle of the contest's run.

Reinforce the goals of the contest or incentive program every day with your staff, using the contest board as a tool to encourage them to do better today than yesterday.

If you want to use the same contest format again because you are pleased with the results, reintroduce it the very next month with a different twist – maybe featuring a different drink item – and present new rewards after 28 days.

Ante Up

If you don't think you have time for complex daily contests, try a round of Sales Poker. It's easy and will keep your servers' morale high and the competitive spirit growing. All you'll need is a deck of poker cards and a prize. First, review your sales record to determine which product area needs a sales boost. Then announce the contest to your staff and name the type of Poker you're going to play – five card draw, perhaps. Shuffle the deck and explain the rules of the game. Say the sales focus is bottles of wine. Servers and bartenders get to draw a card for each bottle they sell over a set minimum. They can also trade one card for another draw, in hopes of improving their hand. The employee with the best hand at the end of the shift takes home the prize.

"When you buy a piece of equipment, you set aside a percentage for maintenance. Shouldn't you do the same for people?"

— William Wiggenborn, President, Motorola University

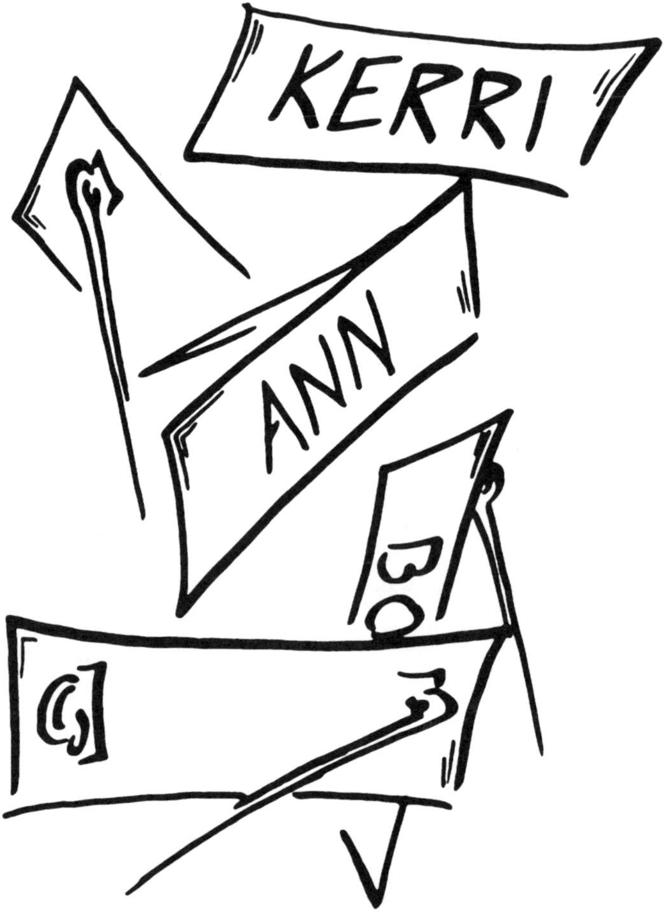

CHAPTER TWO: THE STAFF

You can't do it alone. While a properly functioning ice machine is important to the well-being of your operation, a well-trained, knowledgeable waitstaff can do far more for your bottom line. It's only through your servers and bartenders that you can best reach your customers. Only your severs and bartenders can convince those customers to order more of your higher-margin drink items — and come back again and again.

At the end of Chapter One we let you in on the proven best techniques for effectively training your staff. In Chapter Two, we'll get to the meat of the matter — everything your servers and bartenders need to know to sell everything behind the bar and provide guests with better service.

Would you know how to operate a corkscrew if no one ever showed you? Many servers say the one reason they don't suggest more bottled wine is because they're afraid to open it in front of their guests. How do you pour the perfect draft beer? What goes best with Frangelico and what the heck is an oatmeal stout? How do you know who *not* to serve? You didn't come out of the womb knowing this information — how do you expect your servers and bartenders to know it?

On the pages that follow, you'll find 18 great training tips on customer service, suggestive selling, product knowledge and responsible alcohol service.

18 Get To Know Me

Using effective icebreakers and getting to know guests

"Sometimes you want to go where everybody knows your name."
— Cheers theme

Today's first-timers are tomorrow's regulars. Hey, even Norm and Cliff had to have been first-timers at *Cheers* once upon a time. But whether guests decide to come back again depends on how your staff treats them that first time they come through the front door.

Teach your servers and bartenders to establish a friendly, comfortable relationship from their very first greeting and to get to know their guests – their names, favorite drinks, favorite food items, hobbies, sports, etc.

Do your servers and bartenders use opening greetings that make guests feel comfortable? Good "icebreakers" set the mood for a memorable dining experience. Teach your servers these tips for effective greetings:

- Opening lines should have nothing to do with the menu or drink list. Don't bother with *"Hi, are you ready to order?"* The goal of every server and bartender is to establish a person-to-person relationship. Talking about the menu immediately prevents achieving that goal.
- Opening lines should be questions that encourage conversation. Treating the guest right means thinking about ways to initiate a dialogue, not a server-dominated monologue – and it's the best way to get to know your guest.
- Get the customer talking by asking open-ended questions, like *"Where are you folks off to all dressed up this evening? ... The ballet? How fun for you ... which*

one?" Now you've got a conversation going. Keep it going until you find out something more about the guests – their names, occupations, where they live, etc. *And* you can begin to suggest items that will complement their evening. "*Well, it's a brisk walk over to the theater. How about a couple of our specialty coffee drinks to keep you warm?"*

- Conversation starters can be anything – children, unique clothing, current events, local events, sports, hobbies, professions, weather or holidays.
- The best conversation starters should not be left to chance, however. At your next sales meeting, break staffers into groups and ask everyone to write down their favorite opening lines. Have each group exchange their lines and practice them in role-playing situations.

The Name Game

How do you find out a guest's name? Ask! Introduce yourself: *"Hi, I'm Laura. What's your name?"* Listen to and then immediately repeat the guest's name out loud: *"Mr. Jones, pleased to meet you!"* Use credit cards to learn guests' names: *"Here's your charge slip, Mr. Jones. Come back and see us!"* Repeat or spell the guest's name to yourself three times – don't move your lips! Ask guests what they do for a living. It's easier to remember a name when it's associated with a profession. Write the guest's name and occupation down on a business card, in a journal or customer Rolodex. Introduce the guest to someone else either directly or indirectly. *"Mr. Jones, this is our server, Sally."*

Knowledge Is Power

Teaching product knowledge

"A well-informed employee is the best salesperson a company can have."
— Edwin J. Thomas

The backbone of successful suggestive selling is product knowledge. Hey, you can't sell what you don't know! How silly does a bartender sound when he or she can't name off all the beers your operation serves? Such ineptness doesn't do much for guests' lasting impressions. Use the following training tips to help your employees learn everything they need to know to sell everything behind the bar:

- Give new employees every specialty drink, beer and wine list your restaurant uses. Before they start training, have them study the menus for a few days. Then give them a comprehensive test that includes each drink's ingredients and price, as well as details on each variety of beer and wine. If an employee scores lower than 95 percent, let him or her try the test again a few days later.

- Once they pass the menu test, have all servers go through a training session with a bartender. During the session, have bartenders provide a breakdown of all the wines, spirits and beers your operation offers. Then, have each new server shadow a shift behind the bar to learn the ins and outs of the bartender's world. There's no better way to learn what's in a drink than to watch one being made. It also gives the server a lot more empathy for what the bartender faces on every shift.

- Make product knowledge training an ongoing part of a server's development. Many of your wine, liquor and beer distributors are happy to present product knowledge waitstaff training sessions when new products are released. They may also offer printed information sheets about their products. Ask them for one copy per staff member and go over it during your next training session.

- Test your staff's product knowledge by throwing pop quizzes before each shift. Before your lunch or dinner rush, have the on-duty manager administer a quick five-question quiz to test servers' knowledge and dialogue. Servers and bartenders should memorize specialty drink recipes and be able to name at least two call brands for each well liquor. They should also be able to name a wine-by-the-glass or microbrew selection to go with each of the day's specials. Track the results and award high-scoring employees at your monthly staff meeting.
- Teach your staff that selling requires more than product knowledge – salespeople need product *wisdom*. Not only should they know everything about a product, they should learn to work selections of that knowledge into an effective sales dialogue.

Cheaters *Do* Prosper

You can help your servers keep all that product knowledge top-of-mind by using a photocopier to reduce your specialty drink, beer and wine lists to hand-held cheat sheets. Have servers write a few helpful product knowledge notes or dialogue examples next to each menu item, then laminate the cards so they'll withstand a server's typical use and abuse. Servers can store these helpful cheat sheets in their apron pockets to keep upselling ideas at their fingertips.

20 Word For Word

Painting pictures with words and phrases

"Words, like eyeglasses, blur everything that they do not make clearer."
— *Joseph Joubert*

Language is a good salesperson's best friend. Which of the following sales pitches would most effectively move you to purchase something: "*What can I getcha*?" or "*Have you had a chance to look over our drink list? We're famous for our margaritas. In particular, I'd recommend our delicious Top Shelf margarita. It's made with Cuervo Gold and a splash of Grand Marnier.*"

Servers can't bring out every drink item to show guests what it looks and tastes like. Instead, they have to describe it — preferably in a way that creates a positive mental picture in the guests' mind.

Train your staffers to use well-chosen adjectives and phrases to paint mouth-watering pictures of what they're suggesting to their guests. For example, "*The Sutter Home Cabernet Sauvignon has a full-bodied, robust flavor that would complement your hand-carved prime rib quite nicely....*"

It's important to get employees to practice using descriptive words and phrases. Write the following list of descriptive words and phrases on a flip chart. Go through the list at monthly sales meetings.

For each word, have a server shout out a drink item that could be described using the word. Circle every word servers could use. (You should be able to circle all of the words on the list!) Then, call on servers to work the words into effective sales dialogue.

Beer:	***Wine:***	***Drinks:***
Ice cold	Featured	Fresh fruit
Smooth	Dry	Frosty
Lighter	Full-bodied	Tropical
American	Popular	Creamy
Frosty mug	Fruity	Unique
Refreshing	Imported	Famous
Golden	Natural	Giant
Imported	Robust	Fresh-squeezed

TIP Tell Me More

Here are a few more effective words, and how they could be used to help servers and bartenders sell more beverage items:

Feature: ***"The Sutter Home Chardonnay is our featured wine by the glass this evening." Or, "We're featuring Midori Margaritas tonight for only $2.50."***

Try: ***"Would you like to try Absolut in that Vodka and Tonic?"***

Popular: ***"Our Electric Long Island Iced Tea is our most popular drink. Can I get you one?"***

Let's Get Physical

Positive body language helps increase sales

"Whenever you dance with the customer, always let them lead."
— Manny Garcia, Florida Restaurateur

Each face has a thousand different expressions. Make sure servers let their guests see only those that are pleasant. In other words: Never lose your showbiz face!

Train your servers to show guests their pearly-whites. It's the quickest, easiest, cheapest way for them to acknowledge guests, show they're pleasant, ready and willing to be of service, and that they like their guests.

The eyes have it. Servers shouldn't just stare at their order pads when they're taking an order. They should make eye contact with their guests. It shows guests that the server is listening and understands – and that their orders will be prepared correctly.

Higher sales and bigger tips is all the proof you need that positive body language is important. Train your servers to lean in toward guests as they listen and take the order. They shouldn't be in a "racing stance" – one foot ahead of the other, pointed away from the table, as if the server were getting ready to run away.

Make sure greeters and servers don't forget the kids. It's easier to make a positive impact on children when the body position is lowered down to their level. A happy kid makes a happy table. A happy table leaves a better tip!

Pointed fingers. Listen to what Mom says: Never point – especially to other co-workers or guests in the dining area. Train your entire staff to know the names of all the service areas, table numbers, and to always use an open-palm gesture instead of pointing fingers.

Servers should keep their hands out of their apron pockets unless they're actively searching for something. Also, conduct a daily uniform inspection to check that employees' uniforms are clean and odor-free. Guests should learn about the drink specials from servers' mouth-watering descriptions – not from the various stains on their uniforms!

The Power of Positive Movement

The Pencom Nod is an important form of body language your servers and bartenders can easily master. Here's how it works. As servers suggest items to their guests – for example, *"Would you like to try Beefeater in that Gin and Tonic?"* – all they have to do is smile and slowly nod their heads up and down. It's a subtle, yet amazing form of body language that coaxes guests into agreeing with server suggestions.

22 Prop Up Your Sales

Train servers and bartenders to use sales props

"All the world's a stage but a restaurant is Broadway."
— *Hap Herndon, Director of Training, Brinker International*

The restaurant business is show business – and your servers and bartenders should never go "on stage" without their props. *Sales* props, that is. What are they? Tools servers and bartenders can use to reinforce their menu suggestions. Examples include table tents, promotional posters, menus, bottles of wine, bottles and tall glasses of beer, reader boards and all your beer, wine and specialty drink menus and lists.

Why bother? Customers buy more when salespeople impact several senses while describing their products. When guests have something appealing to look at as a drink item is described, odds are they'll buy it. The key to using sales props is to make sure customers look at them. Oh, and be sure they're clean and in good shape, not stained, frayed or torn.

Here are a few effective ways to teach your servers and bartenders to use their sales props:

- At a pre-shift or monthly sales meeting, have staff practice handing table tents, beer, wine and specialty drink lists to guests and point out specific items as they suggest them. For example, when a guest asks "*What kind of wines do you have?*" servers should open the wine list, hand it to the guest and say: "*We have a great selection, as you'll see here on our wine list. Today we're featuring our Sutter Home wines. They make a terrific Chardonnay which would complement all of the entrees you've ordered (pointing to that item on the list). Shall I bring you a bottle?"* It will help servers reinforce what they *say* with what the guest *sees* to increase sales.

- Look around your restaurant. Are reader boards readable from every table? Have servers and bartenders practice pointing out the ones closest to their section as they describe specials to their guests.
- Hold a staff practice parade around the restaurant, with servers and bartenders carrying trays with bottles of wine, eye-appealing drinks, tall beers, appetizers and desserts through the dining room in a way that will catch the most customer attention. This is one of the most effective techniques for selling eye-appealing drinks and desserts — that's why servers should always remember to make a show of delivering them each time a customer orders one.

Saving the Best for Last

Consider adding small "airline-size" liqueur bottles to your dessert tray. That way, when servers display the tray to their guests, they'll automatically remember to suggest after-dinner drinks, as well as dessert and liqueur combinations. Train them to keep the tray below the guest's eye level and point out each dessert and liqueur while describing it. It's a great, inexpensive way to increase your sales of specialty liqueurs. But instead of actually serving those small bottles, fill the display bottles with water to control inventory and pour from the big bottles at the bar — it's much cheaper.

23 To Sell Is To Serve

Sales techniques to move everything on the menu

"A salesperson is someone who sells goods that won't come back to customers who will."
— Anonymous

If you want your servers to move more of your bar items, you have to prepare them with effective sales techniques they can use in all different selling situations. You can help by teaching them the following:

- Say it first and last. People tend to remember the first and last things you say so mention the item you want to sell twice – in general at first, then more specific at the end of the dialogue. Advertisers have been using this technique for years – and it really works! To sell more beer, say, *"Can I get you something to drink? A frosty mug of ice cold beer, a glass of wine, a cocktail? Today we're featuring drafts of Big Nose Red Ale."*

- Assume the sale. It's not being pushy, it's just being confident. You may hear "no thanks" when you suggest a bottle of wine with dinner, but that doesn't mean you shouldn't try again with your next table. Listen to the assumption in the following dialogue: *"Can I bring you another beer now, or would you like to wait until I bring your sandwiches?"* Works nearly every time.

- Always offer a choice. In many cases, people have only the words on the menu and the server's dialogue to help them make decisions. So it's up to the server or bartender to give the guest an "overview." One way is to suggest at least two choices of everything. For example, "*Would you like to try Bombay or Tanqueray in your gin and tonic?*"

- Features and Benefits. Your servers should know menu items in terms of features – *what is it?* – and benefits – *what will it do for the guest?* Reciting the features and benefits of an item when making helpful suggestions makes it easier to sell that item. Take an Amaretto specialty coffee drink, for example:

Features	Benefits
It's only $2.75	That's less than coffee and dessert
It's topped with fresh whipped cream	It has less fat than a regular dessert
A side of Amaretto is just $1 extra	An amaretto normally costs $2
You can get it to-go	It's great for rushed guests
We use fresh, imported ingredients	It's the best in town

Tune In to the Occasion

Special occasions can be anything – a birthday, anniversary or job promotion. Just listen to your guests. Say, for example, you hear "*Our boss gave us the rest of the day off.*" A good salesperson's line would be, *"Hey, congratulations! Sounds like you guys are ready to do some celebrating. How about a few cold beers, some champagne – or perhaps one of our great specialty drinks. Our Electric Iced Tea will knock your socks off!"*

24 The King of Sales

Upselling beer

"Cliff: Hey, Norm, how does a beer sound?

Norm: Pretty quiet 'til four in the morning."

— *Cheers*

Drinking beer is one of the world's oldest pastimes. With food or by itself, it's the most popular adult beverage in the U.S. In fact, people drink more beer than wine and distilled spirits combined.

So selling beer to a thirsty guest should be as easy as — well — selling beer to a thirsty guest! But despite the easy sale, the beer trade comes with a few costly negatives: kegs take up space, bottles must be stocked, all of it must be kept cold — make that *ice* cold — to ward off customer complaints and all those empties take up space in the garbage or recycling bin.

That's why it's important for servers to upsell at every turn. Here are a few techniques and dialogue examples you can teach your staff:

- Have servers and bartenders suggest beer as part of their opening dialogue: *"How about a frosty mug of Bud or Bud Light to get you started?"*
- Keep bottles of beer selections prominently displayed (and dust free) on the back bar, but be sure servers can recite them by name, instead of just pointing above the bar when a guest inquires about the selection.
- If you offer pitchers, servers should always suggest a trade-up when two or more customers at the same table ask for a draft: *"We're featuring a great deal on our Bud Draft today: A pitcher for $3.95 will save you $1.50."*

- If you sell two sizes, train servers to automatically nod their head up and down while saying *"Large?"*
- Sell bottled beer by "the bucket" at a special price.
- Use key words like "feature," "icy" and "cold": *"We're featuring ice-cold Budweiser and Miller Lite on tap. Either will taste great with your hot wings and pizza!"*
- List beers brewed in the United States as "American" not "domestic." It sounds better: *"We have a great selection of American beers. Today we're featuring Bud, Samuel Adams, Coors Light and O'Doul's. Which can I get for you?"*
- To sell a second pitcher of beer to groups of four or more, always "assume" the sale: *"Would you like me to bring you another pitcher of beer now, or with your entrees?"*
- Always compliment your guest's order: *"A pitcher of Michelob? Great choice!"*

Perfect Pairing

Pair up beers with specific appetizers at a special price and train servers to mention the special during their opening dialogue with guests. For example, *"Tonight we're featuring a pitcher of Bud Light and our Ultimate Nachos for only $6.95!"* List the pairings on your menu, daily special sheet or on table tents and train servers and host staff to point them out to guests. Use colorful table tents on every table and at every other bar stool that feature and highlight the beers you offer, as well as beer and appetizer specials. Check them daily to make sure they are clean and in tip-top condition.

25 Clean Up Your Act

The secrets of a "beer-clean" glass

"I never have more than one drink before dinner. But I do like that one to be very large and very strong and very cold and very well-made."

— James Bond, Ian Fleming's Casino Royale

Beer drinkers aren't a picky bunch. They just want every draft to look just right – with the perfect head and a foamy ring left on the glass after every sip – and taste just right – cold, crisp and lively. And they're typically very loyal to their brand of choice, so they know when something's gone awry. One screw-up and you could lose the guest forever.

It's a tough trade, since so much can go wrong with draft beer: Flatness could be caused by a greasy glass, a loose tap or leaky pressure. Cloudy beer comes from an over-chilled keg or hot spots in the keg line. Wild beer is caused by improper pouring, worn faucets, twists or obstructions in the lines. And funny tastes come from dirty faucets, beer lines – even dirty, oily air in the kitchen or bar. Makes you wonder how you'll *ever* get one right. One way is to make sure your kegs, lines and faucets are properly maintained.

The other is to train all your servers and bartenders the five steps to ensure "beer-clean" glasses, since a clean glass is essential to pouring the perfect looking and tasting beer. That glass is the last link between a finely brewed beer and your customer.

- Start with a clean three-compartment sink: Sink one should be filled with warm water and glass cleaner, and should feature an overflow pipe to maintain a constant water level and a funnel strainer to catch residue when glasses are emptied. Number two should be filled with cool water, with a slow but steady stream allowed to run throughout the washing operation. Number three is filled with sanitizer and clean cool water.

- Empty all contents into the funnel in sink one. Scrub vigorously using a low-suds glass-cleaning detergent and, wherever possible, motorized brushes. Use odor-free, nonfat cleaning compounds made especially for cleaning beer glasses. Oil-based detergents can leave a film.
- Thoroughly rinse glasses in sink two. Always place the glass bottom down in the rinse to eliminate the chance of air pockets forming and/or improper rinsing.
- Repeat in sink three.
- Air dry by placing glass upside down on a deeply corrugated drain board, allowing air to enter the inverted glass and complete the drying operation by evaporation.

Throw Out the Towel

Train your staff never to dry glasses with a towel or place them on top of a cloth on the bar or countertop to dry. Bleaches and detergents often leave a residue on towels and wash rags. That residue can release fumes into the glass that will spoil beer's delicate flavor. If stubborn stains require scrubbing with a cloth, that glass must be washed and rinsed again.

26 Pour Control

Don't let your staff pour away your beer profits

"The restaurant business is the only business in which there are more ways to lose money than to make money."
— John "Doc" Gardner

There are many, many ways to lose money in the restaurant and bar business. And one of your worst money drains is your draft beer faucet. Sure, draft beers provide some of the best margins behind the bar — but it's easy to picture why sometimes you still end up losing money. Imagine turning that faucet on and walking away for a few minutes. See those dollar bills going down the drain? Yet many operators still let it happen, erroneously thinking that they're "warming up" the lines for a good draw.

Truth is the old practice of opening the line before pouring is unnecessary and wasteful. Operators who employ this practice risk losing five to 10 percent of their beer profits every year. If you find you do need to "warm up" your lines, it could mean they need to be cleaned or your beer isn't cold enough.

And that all-important head on top of the beer is another source for profit and loss. Foam is about 25 percent liquid beer. Beer drinkers expect there to be about an inch of it at the top. Any more or less and they think they're getting ripped off. If there's too much foam, they *are* getting scammed. But if there's no foam, they're actually getting *more* for their money, which means a loss for the operator. Beer served in a 10-ounce hourglass with a one-inch head yields 264 glasses from a half-barrel. The same 10-ounce glass of beer, minus the head, yields only 198 glasses. That's a loss of 66 glasses. At $1 gross margin per glass, there is $66 more gross profit in every half-barrel when beer is properly served. Teach your bar staff these tips for pouring the perfect beer in terms of both taste and profits:

- Start with a clean glass dipped in cold water. Never use a warm glass or one that hasn't been cleaned, rinsed and drained properly. The slightest residue will ruin the head and flatten the beer.
- Place the glass at an angle about one inch below the faucet. Open the faucet quickly, all the way. Never let the rim of the glass touch the faucet.
- Fill the glass to half-full, gradually bringing it to an upright position. Let the remaining beer run down the middle. This ensures a three-quarter-inch to one-inch head – your source of profit. When pouring pitchers, try for a one- to one-and-a-half-inch head.
- If you have an order for several drinks including a draft, always pour the beer last just before the server delivers the orders. If poured first, it may lose its head before reaching the customer. And never use a swizzle stick or straw to bring back the head.

Stout Traditions

There's one exception to the "last-pour" rule. Heavy stouts, like Guinness for example, come out very slow and create a thick, creamy foam that takes time to settle. Train bartenders to pour stouts first and let them sit for a few minutes while preparing the other drinks. The foam will slowly work its way up the glass, leaving the thick, almost-black liquid at the bottom. Once the foam line reaches about three quarters up the glass, just top it off leaving an inch or so of foam on top. Don't worry about it getting warm – stouts are best served at about 55 degrees. And don't apologize for the delay – stout drinkers are used to the ritual, so they won't mind waiting the few extra minutes.

27 Heads Up

Product knowledge is the key to selling hand-crafted beers

It's tough to find a bar or restaurant these days that doesn't serve at least one variety of microbrew or specialty beer. They're enormously popular and easy to sell since, unlike your loyal-to-one-brand domestic beer drinkers, microbrew buffs love to try something new.

But it's not worth stocking a selection if you can't get your servers to sell it. That's where product knowledge can help. Share the following "microbrew basics" with your staff to help them make suggestions to your guests.

There are hundreds of different specialty brands in the world, but most fall under two categories: ales and lagers.

Ale is the older style, steeped in English tradition. Its fruity aroma and robust flavor is created by using top-fermenting yeasts near room temperature – which is why ales are best when not refrigerated. Some classic styles include:

- Pale Ale. Actually not pale at all, but bronze or amber, Pale Ale was named to distinguish it from the much darker brews of its day. You'll often hear of India Pale Ales, named for when the British brewed stiffer batches to survive the long journey to their troops in distant lands.
- Porter. Technically in the ale family, but this dark brew's potent taste puts it in a category all its own.
- Stout. The darker big brother of the Porter, although it's not necessarily higher in alcohol. You're likely to find Sweet Stouts, Oatmeal Stouts, even Oyster Stouts.

"It was as natural as eating and to me as necessary, and I would not have thought of eating a meal without drinking ... beer."
— Ernest Hemingway

Unlike an ale, a lager uses bottom-fermenting yeasts at lower temperatures. Longer maturation results in a crisper, more thirst-quenching beer. There are two types that get the most attention:

- Pilsner. The most popular variety of lager worldwide. Golden, clear and light with a flowery aroma and refreshing carbonation, it's what most people picture when they think of beer.
- Bock. A very strong lager, full-bodied but still very smooth. Its strong, almost burnt flavor makes it a brew you may not want to recommend to someone new to microbrews.

A rule of thumb: Taste is subjective, but a good tip in making recomendations is the darker the food, the darker the beer. A lighter-colored food like baked chicken might go well with a Golden Pilsner or Light Ale. But add some spicy barbecue sauce, throw it on the grill and that chicken would probably go better with a Porter.

More on Micros

There are a few additional styles of specialty beers emerging in the marketplace that you and your staff should know about:

- **Wheat is added to barley during brewing to create the refreshing Wheat Beer. Its thirst-quenching flavor is even better with a wedge of fresh lemon.**
- **Fruit beers are tantalizing taste buds everywhere. It's not uncommon to find beers flavored with cherries, blueberries, apricots, raspberries, cranberries, lemons – even chili peppers.**
- **Steam beer is a decidedly American invention. It uses a lager yeast fermented at an ale yeast temperature. The result is the best of both worlds – the smooth drinkability of a lager with the fruity robustness of an ale.**

28 Breaking Tradition

Recommending wines by the bottle

"It's a naive domestic Burgundy without any breeding, but I think you'll be amused by its presumption."
—James Thurber

Over the years, the traditional pomp and circumstance that goes along with selling and serving wine has come to work against it in sales. Sure, at fine-dining establishments bottled wine sales are still the norm, but in more casual restaurants people are often too intimidated by wine's sometimes ostentatious traditions.

And it's not always the *customers'* fears that are the problem. For most operators, the biggest hindrance to increased bottled wine sales is the inexperienced server too intimidated to make suggestions from the wine list. Break the mystique by teaching your waitstaff the basics of wine and how to make simple, low-pressure suggestions that would complement the guests' meals.

Wine sales training will be welcome to all your servers once you explain that selling just one bottle to every fourth four-top per shift could increase their tips by $2,000 this year. It also helps the server save time, since he or she won't need to run back and forth for additional wines by the glass.

And helpful suggestions are welcome to your non-wine-connoisseur guests if they're presented in a friendly, non-threatening way. Start by explaining to your staff what type of wine goes with the main food items on your menu:

Appetizers	Champagne, dry white, sherry
Beef, Lamb	Hearty red
Poultry, Seafood, Veal	Dry or medium white, rosé

The ground rule is simply red wine with red meat and white wine with white meat or seafood. National wines often complement national cuisine. So a good choice with Lasagna, for instance, would be a Red Chianti. Greek wine really only tastes right next to Greek food. And there are few wines that will hold up alongside highly spiced food. Spicy enchiladas, for example, are best accompanied by a frozen margarita.

These days, though, there's plenty of room for personal preference. Customers should never be made to feel foolish for trying new things. Advise servers to make recommendations based on the traditional rules, but if a customer decides on something else, let there be no raised eyebrows — let there only be "*That's an excellent choice, sir.*" No matter how peculiar the guest's taste may seem, reaffirming his choice could spur another sale on a return visit next week.

A Sweet Treat

One of the most overlooked times to suggest wine is at the end of the meal. Because we already know that wine and food pairings naturally make both taste better, it makes perfect sense to teach your staff about the exquisite taste sensations of these dessert and wine combinations:

- **Dry cabernet and chocolate**
- **Sparkling wine and fresh fruit (especially strawberries)**
- **Port wine and any dessert with nuts (especially walnuts and hazelnuts)**

We Will Sell No Wine...

Training servers to sell and upsell wine

Actually, there are many opportunities to suggest and sell wine during every meal — and many ways servers can effectively upsell. Why wait until it's "time"?

"We will sell no wine before its time."
— Ernest and Julio Gallo

Train servers to use these four specific opportunities to suggest wine during every meal:

1. During the initial greeting of the table.
2. When the entree order is taken.
3. In the period between soup and salad and serving the main course.
4. When the entrees are delivered, suggest a specific wine to complement their particular dish.

Tell servers to keep in mind that people usually remember the first and last things they say. Have them mention wine in general at the beginning of the sales dialogue, then get specific at the end. For example: "*Can I start you off with some wine, a beer or a cocktail? Tonight we're featuring our Sutter Home Chardonnay by the glass.*"

Teach servers to always suggest mid-priced wines to guests unless they specifically ask for a premium vintage. It builds customer confidence — which builds repeat traffic.

Remind servers that when two or more guests order a glass of the same wine during the initial greeting, they should suggest a bottle. For example: "*Since you're both having a glass of the Sutter Home White Zinfandel, why not share a bottle? You'll each get about two glasses and save a few dollars."*

Assign each server and bartender specific daily wine sales goals before each shift. Reward achievers with a draw from a bowl of $1 state lottery tickets.

Or contact your wine vendors to provide merchandise (T-Shirts, wine glasses, racks, key chains, etc.) for a month-long sales contest. Consider doubling the incentive at lunch since it's usually harder to sell wine then.

Wine Patrol

Need to boost wine sales? Savvy operators everywhere are trying new techniques to increase sales. One chain keeps a jug of house wine on every table, charging guests on the "honor system." Another dubs one server "wine patrol" for the shift. Typically the operation's wine expert, this server isn't assigned a regular section, but moves through tables with an open bottle of a featured wine and several inverted glasses. As guests review their menus, they're offered a complimentary taste. If there's an interest, wine patrol describes the wine and menu items it complements – and answers questions about other wines on the list. After the tasting, those who request a full glass are served right away. If a bottle is ordered, the wine patrol is the one to fetch, open and pour, saving other servers time while earning big tips!

30 Have No Fear

Training servers to open and pour wine

"Nothing worth learning is learned quickly except parachuting."

— Christopher O'Donnell, Denver restaurant manager

For many servers, the biggest fear about selling wine is that they may have to open and serve it *in front of all those people!* To get servers more comfortable selling it, you'll need to get them more comfortable with the age-old process of opening and presenting it. Teach them the following wine presentation tips:

- Carry the bottle motionless with the bottom in the upturned palm, the back resting on the forearm, so the bottle top sits at a 30-degree angle.
- Present the bottle from the host's right to avoid reaching in front of him or her when pouring and identify the wine aloud: "*Sutter Home Cabernet Sauvignon*."
- Open the bottle on a tabletop or in an ice bucket. It's less distracting than opening it in-hand.
- Cut the foil under the lower lip about a half inch from the mouth to prevent dripping and contamination from lead. Place the foil in your apron pocket.
- Wipe a damp napkin along the top – even if it looks clean, wiping it will ease any customer concerns.
- Insert the corkscrew so the spiral's hollow center is at the center of the cork. Turn until the spiral disappears. Hold the fulcrum on the lip and pull the cork out. Remove the cork from the spiral and place it on a napkin to the host's right. Without pausing, wipe the mouth clean and pour the host an ounce or two to sample.

- If the host, due to inexperience, doesn't taste the sample, ask with a smile, "*Would you care to taste the wine?*" If not, or after he or she does and gives approval, serve the guests, ladies first, before returning to complete the host's pour. Circle in a clockwise direction so you won't have to change directions at each guest's side.
- With napkin in opposite hand, begin the pour briskly. Lowering the bottle too slowly causes wine to dribble down the side of the bottle. Twisting the wrist during the upward motion can prevent dripping. Pour each glass about two-thirds full, taking care that you don't touch the rim of the glass with the bottle.
- Place red wines on a coaster or underliner within reach of the host's right hand, label facing him or her. Place chilled wines in an ice bucket, also within reach of the host's right hand, with a cloth napkin attached to or laid across the top.
- If a second bottle is ordered, bring a clean glass only for the host's sample. Remove it as soon as it is empty.

Be Prepared

Let servers practice opening wine until it seems effortless – both to servers *and* guests. Consider letting staffers open your "house" wines daily for your bartender. Your wine vendors may also be able to supply you with "dummy" or practice bottles to work with during team meetings. Each server should have his or her own wine opener for every shift. Inspect daily during the uniform check or pre-shift team meetings. Keep an extra supply on hand for staff members who "lost" or "forgot" their openers. You can either "rent" them for, say, $5 a shift (be sure to get them back!), or sell them outright for $20 to servers or bartenders who forgot theirs.

31 Say What?

Wine pronunciation guide

Another important part of selling wine is the ability to pronounce the names of all your wines. Nothing makes a guest lose confidence more than a server who struggles with pronunciation. Hey, communication is half the battle! If servers know how to present wine suggestions with confidence, the guests will trust their expertise. Use the key below to help employees practice the most common wine names.

"Your competition is not your competition. Your competition is the competency level of your salespeople."
— Tom Peters

Bordeaux	bore-DOUGH
Burgundy	BURR-gun-dee
Cabernet Sauvignon	cab-air-NAY so-veen-YOWN
Chablis	shuh-BLEE
Chardonnay	shar-dah-NAY
Chenin Blanc	SHEH-nen BLAHNK
Chianti	key-YAWN-tee
French Colombard	French COL-LUM-bard
Gamay Beaujolais	Gah-MAY bo-zhuh-LAY
Gewurtztraminer	guh-VOORTZ-tram-mee-nair
Grenache	gruh-NAHSH
Merlot	mare-LOW
Petit Sirah	pe-TEET seer-AAH
Pinot Grigio	PEE-no GREE-zhee-o

Pinot Noir	PEE-no N'wahr
Riesling	REESE-ling
Rosé	row-ZAY
Sauvignon Blanc	so-veen-YOWN BLAHNK
Zinfandel	ZIN-fan-del

At your next monthly sales training meeting, break employees into small groups (about two or three people) and pass out sets of flashcards with all the wines' names, phonetic spellings, features, benefits and prices written on them. Instruct groups to practice pronouncing each wine's name, then discuss its price, features and benefits and what menu items it would complement. Bring the group back together and go through the list once more, having all staff say the names out loud. Then call on individuals to describe the wine. Write all the responses on a flip chart. Later, have several employees role-play making wine recommendations to their guests.

Business As Usual

Try this role-play scenario at your next training session to get servers more comfortable suggesting wine: *It's lunchtime. Four business people are intensely discussing work. How could you suggest wine to these guests?* Manager's key: Make sure your employees aren't afraid to suggest wine at lunch. Encourage them to ask questions — Are they done for the day? Need to go to a long meeting after lunch? Celebrating a promotion? Closing a big deal? Your operation should feature a lighter wine at lunchtime to go along with salads, pastas and sandwiches. A non-alcohol wine may also be an appropriate suggestion.

32 Something Special

Selling specialty drinks

What's the point in ordering and stocking all those funky drink mixes and garnishes for unique specialty drinks if servers don't suggest and sell them? But suggesting just the right kinds of specialty drinks to the right people can be an art form. But it is the perfect way to ensure guests have a great time and leave a better tip.

"I am the world's worst salesman, therefore I must make it easy for people to buy."
— Frank W. Woolworth

Teach your servers to wow guests by suggesting specialty drinks in mouth-watering detail. Here are a few examples:

- Suggest tequila-based drinks to go with Southwestern or Mexican-themed foods. For example, *"How about a margarita or one of our famous Tequila Matadors to go with your Southwest Sirloin? The Matador is made with gold tequila, pineapple juice, a splash of fresh lime and it's served over crushed ice in a champagne flute."*
- Appeal to your guest's desire to try something "off the beaten track." Instead of the standard glass of wine, suggest a refreshing wine drink. For example, *"The Asian Chicken Salad is an excellent choice. I recommend a white wine to go with it. If you want something really special, try our White Bellini. It's made with peach juice, sparkling white wine, a dash of black currant juice and a dash of lemon juice. It's a real taste treat!"*
- Don't serve boring old coffee to every guest. Instead suggest coffee specialty drinks to every table. For example, "*Would you like to try one of our famous iced coffee drinks? They're just the thing to take the heat*

off. The Icy Fudge Sludge granita is very popular. It's a frosty shake made with mocha cappuccino, rippled with hot fudge and whipped cream. But my favorite is the Iced Raspberry-Vanilla Latté. It's very tasty."

- Suggest wine-based drinks for something special on warm nights. For example, "*We have an excellent choice of wines. And for something a little different, I suggest a Kir Royale. It's three ounces of premium champagne and a splash of creme de cassis.*"
- If parties of three or four order the same soft drink, suggest "group" drinks or the beverage by the pitcher. For example, "*Since you're all getting the cherry cola, you may want to try our one-and-only Cherry Bomb. It's cherry cola served in a huge 'fishbowl' you all can share, garnished with dry ice, cherry ice cubes and a splash of grenadine. It's a lot more fun to drink than a plain glass of cola – and you get to keep the container!*"

Today's Specials

A few more tips for selling specialty drinks:

- **Create drama drinks by using dry ice to make them bubble and fun garnishes like wacky straws or huge fruit wheels.**
- **Use appealing glassware that's unique to your restaurant – then parade the drinks around and watch them sell themselves.**
- **Have a "Customer Specialty Drink Recipe Contest" to fill your recipe book with new drink ideas. Offer contest winners a gift certificate and name the drink after them.**

33 Tiny Bubbles

Tips on selling and serving champagne

No celebration is complete without a little bubbly. And selling champagne will keep operators celebrating since the margins can be so good. Guests don't go through the usual price hesitation when they're feeling festive.

"My God ... it's full of stars!"

— Dom Pèrignon, the blind Benedictine monk and cellarmaster who developed champagne, upon his first taste in 15th-century France

But most operators hesitate stocking quantities of champagne because too often it sits in the racks until the beginning of the Christmas season.

The mindset that people won't buy champagne year-round isn't necessarily true. And it begins with your waitstaff. Teach servers and bartenders to suggest and sell champagne all year round — you never know when an ordinary date will turn into a celebration.

Train everyone answering the phone to "pre-sell" bottles of wine or champagne when guests call to make reservations for special events. For example, "*You'd like to make a reservation for an anniversary party for a group of 10? Great! Would you like us to have a few bottles of champagne chilling tableside when you arrive*?"

Suggest special champagne and dessert pairings. For example, "*Tonight we're featuring a glass of our featured champagne with every item on our dessert tray for a special price. It's a great value.*"

A good way to sell a second bottle of champagne is to assume the sale. As you pour out the remainder of the first bottle into your party's glass, ask, "*Would you like me to bring you another bottle of champagne now or would you like to wait until I bring your entrees?"*

For guests who may be the designated driver or choose not to have an alcohol beverage, suggest a sparkling cider or non-alcohol wine. *"Instead of coffee, if you'd like, I could bring you a glass of our great-tasting non-alcohol white wine. It's really popular."* It's a special treat for children, too — they'll love raising their sparking grape juice glass in toast along with their parents.

Offer champagne and menu pairings. Most popular is the all-in-one-price weekend brunch that includes either Bloody Mary's, Champagne or Mimosas. But be creative. Another combination may better suit your establishment.

Presenting and Serving Champagne

Cradle the bottle with the label out as you carry it to the table. Present it to the host, repeating its name. Remove foil and place a napkin over the cork. Grip the cork firmly, gently twist and pull the bottle away from you. The cork shouldn't make a "pop!" sound when it releases. Holding the bottle from the base with your thumb in the punt, pour the host a one-quarter-inch sample. After approval, pour clockwise around the table to ladies first, gentlemen second, the host last. Fill each glass no more than two-thirds full, taking care not to touch the bottle to the glass. Avoid dripping by using a smooth twist-and-pull motion. Use good judgment with large parties — make sure everyone gets some. Place the bottle in the bucket near the host. Leave the napkin so the host can remove the bottle without dripping. Be sure to suggest a second bottle!

To Top It Off

Selling after dinner drinks

After-dinner drinks are a promising area of sales opportunity for your servers. And they're easy to sell since many guests will order these sweet delights along with their dessert — or in place of dessert to save a few calories. The down-side is there are so many varieties out there, inventory can get a little sticky.

"Candy is dandy, but liquor is quicker."
— Ogden Nash

If you're going to stock them, you're going to have to get your servers and bartenders to sell them. The following sales tips and dialogue examples should help:

- Display a list of liqueur-coffee-dessert combinations either on a menu or table tent for guests to look over. Be sure servers have the list memorized and consistently recommend combinations to guests in mouth-watering terms.

- Train servers to always suggest an after-dinner drink before suggesting coffee. For example, "*Would you like to try one of our great after-dinner drinks? We have a Kahlua latte that's delicious. We also have a Cognac Martini that's excellent!*"

- Servers should automatically suggest coffee as a companion drink to a cordial. For example, "*Would you like a cup of coffee to go with your Chambord?*"

- Teach servers which drinks go with which types of coffees and desserts. Hold a training meeting where servers can sample drinks in combination with dessert samples. Ask them to describe the flavors. For example, *"Your Chocolate Torte would taste great with a Bailey's Irish Cream – and the Frangelico is superb with the Hazelnut Cheesecake."*

- Servers should always recommend their personal favorites. For example, *"My favorite is the Amaretto Coffee with the Pecan Pie and Brandy ice cream. We also have a wide variety of excellent cheesecakes, too."*
- Servers should tune in to the occasion. For example, if a party of two looks tense, chances are they won't be staying for after-dinner drinks. But if they seem to be celebrating a special occasion, your guests may want to linger over a tasty after-dinner cordial. For example, *"You look like you're celebrating a special occasion. Would you like to share a special dessert-for-two? We have a great dessert called Cupid's Cake made with layers of strawberries, whipped cream and chocolate. It's perfect with a toast of Chambord!"*

Double Play

Teach servers to go for a double upsell when they suggest desserts and after-dinner drinks. For instance, *"As you see on the menu, we have some great liqueur and dessert combinations. The homemade vanilla ice cream is great with Kahlua drizzled on top!"* If a guest orders a piece of Hot Apple Pie, a server could not only recommend it á la mode, but also with a shot of butterscotch schnapps over the ice cream. Or, if a guest wants a bowl of fresh fruit in season, the server might suggest it tossed with a shot of Grand Marnier or Chambord. Guests that may not have ordered an after-dinner drink can easily be encouraged by the elegant upgrade of a simple dessert.

35 Faking It

Responsible alcohol service and ID checking

There's a new kind of art form emerging from today's high schools, and every night at your bar or restaurant a server will come across one of its best works. Today's fake IDs look more realistic than ever. Are you confident that your server will be able to detect it and refuse service to a minor? Stakes are high. Be sure to train, test, re-train and test again all of your bartenders and servers until you're sure they're well-versed in the principles of ID checking and responsible alcohol service. Here are a few training tips:

"Oh, I don't carry an ID. I'm a priest, my son."
— One anonymous underage drinker's inventive excuse

- Penalties can shut down your operation, not only due to expensive lawsuits, fines and liquor license suspension, but also through lost business due to bad publicity. Be sure servers and bartenders know the penalties that could affect *them* if they serve a minor — their own fines, criminal punishment and often termination of employment.
- Teach servers and bartenders to card everyone who appears to be under 30 — and make it your policy not to serve *anyone* under 30 who can't produce a valid ID.
- Be sure your servers and bartenders are familiar with the four basic types of fake IDs and how to detect them: 1. Altered: IDs in which the photo, birth date or expiration date have been changed using a cut and paste method. They're the most common — and can be spotted by holding them up to light and looking for cut lines, bumps or changes in the type. 2. Counterfeit: They look official but generally don't match the size, shape and

style of a valid ID. In an age of high-tech computer graphics, IDs can be counterfeited more easily and more convincingly than ever. Counterfeits can be hard to catch, but inevitably something will set them apart from those in your ID checking guide. 3. Forged: These are made from stolen license blanks so they do match size, shape and style but won't have the official validation stamp. They're very hard to detect and should be checked carefully against your ID checking guide. 4. False impersonation: When someone assumes the ID of someone else by actually duplicating the ID at the motor vehicles office or by using someone else's ID. Just be sure IDs are removed from wallets and plastic, examined in proper light, carefully compared with the person and scrutinized for discrepancies in physical appearance.

- Once you've taught servers all the ins and outs of ID checking, test their skills through role-playing exercises. Just like opening wine bottles, many servers are uncomfortable asking customers for IDs. Training will help them become more comfortable.

New Kids on the Block

Body language can be a dead-giveaway when it comes to determining a minor's true age. Train servers to watch for these tell-tale signs:

Eyes: **Avoids eye contact, looks down or around the room.**

Voice: **Nervous, high or trying to sound deep; sometimes loud and giggly.**

Behavior: **Overly friendly; tries to remain inconspicuous; asks prices; sometimes pools money with friends before ordering; doesn't know what to order or orders sweet drinks like daiquiris and margaritas.**

"The secret to operating a successful bar: Get 'em up, get 'em thirsty, set 'em down, let 'em drink!"

— Clint Hughes, VP Strategic Marketing & National Accounts, Harborage I, Ltd.

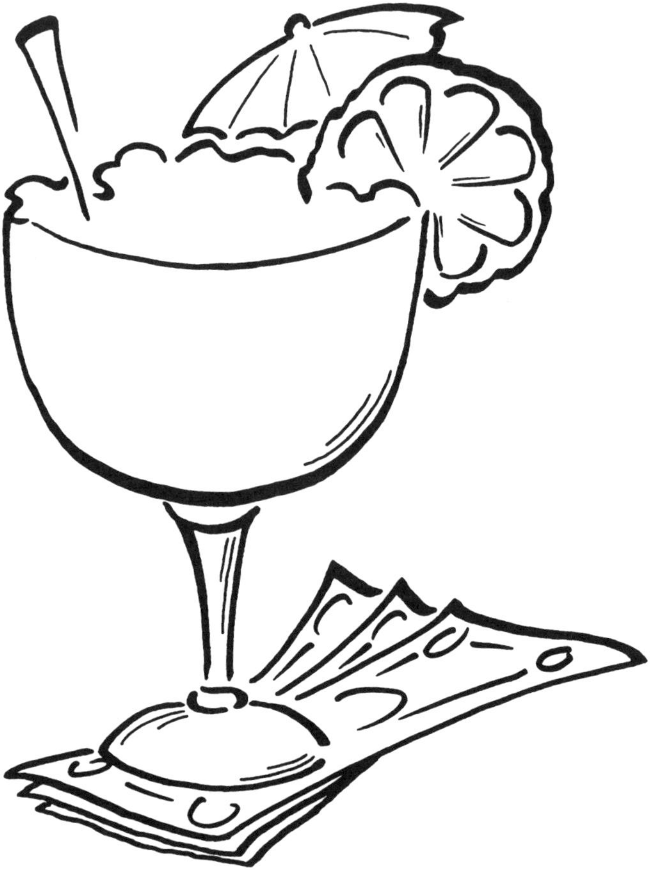

CHAPTER THREE: THE CUSTOMER

How does an ordinary restaurant or bar operation become the local hot spot? Truth is, it can't. There's nothing *ordinary* about an operation that can continually pack the house in today's competitive marketplace. But you can increase your chances with an effective mix of marketing, customer service and value for the dollar. A little positive word-of-mouth advertising doesn't hurt, either.

But becoming "*the* place to be" is something you have to strive for – because all your competitors are going after the same thing. Effective marketing isn't just running a two-for-one happy hour promotion once in a while. It's a day-in, day-out concern of all successful bar and restaurant managers – a unique combination of internal and external forces that come together to create a positive customer perception. And it has to be carefully planned.

On the following pages are 17 great ideas on evaluating your place in the market, developing a marketing plan for the year, designing effective POS and promotional materials and presenting effective promotions with help from your staff and your suppliers.

From the Inside Out

Creating an atmosphere where guests want to come back again and again

"Great marketing can kill a bad business."
— Dan Dains

There are a lot of marketing schemes bar and restaurant operators use to get customers through the front door: television advertising, expensive promotions, big banners outside. But convincing those customers to come back depends on the service they receive.

Many operations neglect the art of customer service because they're too busy throwing money at advertising. But it's the competence of the staff – not external marketing schemes – that determines the level of repeat business.

That big advertising budget is wasted if those guests are subjected to lazy, indifferent or unfriendly service. If bad service drives them away, no amount of advertising will motivate them to come back.

To turn a first-time customer into a regular – the guy that never misses a Friday happy hour, the couple that dines at your place every Saturday night – focus your efforts on internal marketing. It's the quality of service that makes people glad they came to a bar or restaurant, makes them want to linger a little over an extra cocktail or after-dinner drink they may not have originally planned on, and makes them want to return often – with their friends.

Train servers and bartenders to go the extra mile with all guests. Welcome them with a smile. Talk to them. Pull out their chairs. Hang up their coats. Learn their names. Treat them all like movie stars.

Set goals for staffers on learning and using guests' names, making advance reservations, doing "little something extras" like drawing a map for guests to use to get to a movie, putting a mug on ice so their next draft will be extra cold or calling guests at home to alert them that their favorite bottled wine will be going on special. Your employees have as much to gain as the operation does, since increased traffic means an increase in their tips.

Relying on advertising alone just doesn't make financial sense for bars and restaurants struggling to succeed in this highly competitive industry. The smart money is on providing quality customer service. It can be the difference between the long-term customer and the one-timer.

Follow the Leader

Your staff will do as much or as little as you lead them to do, so you'd better lead the way. Set a good example whenever you work the floor. Greet guests, shake their hands, hang up their coats. Make menu suggestions. Upsell the way you'd like your staff to upsell. Your staff will take notice and follow suit. Set personal mini-marketing goals for yourself on every shift. They may be as simple as learning and using two new guests' names, getting two business cards, and then following up on those cards with a personal (always hand-written!) thank you note for their patronage.

37 Risk Breaking

Creating a marketing plan

> **"If your don't know where you are going, you will probably not wind up there."**
> — ***Forrest Gump***

Why take the chance that your marketing efforts will fail? By creating a plan that integrates all your marketing efforts and sets your entire operation toward a common goal, you won't be taking any chances. You'll give your operation a set track to run on by creating a stable, planning-oriented framework. You'll be able to place your operation's potential into perspective by analyzing your competition as well as your own operation. You'll be able to realistically rank your priorities, assign responsibilities and designate deadlines while removing any guesswork. And, in the long run, you'll probably find yourself ahead of your competition.

But effectively constructing a marketing plan takes an enormous amount of forethought. Here are some questions you should answer before you begin:

- Who are my target customers?
- What are the basic strengths of my operation?
- What needs do my customers have?
- Who is my competition?
- How effective are my current marketing efforts?
- Do I have the financial and human resources I need to support my marketing efforts?

With your answers, you're ready to begin. Here's how to develop a marketing plan in seven basic steps:

1 Market Research: Find out exactly what your customers think of your operation.

2 Use that information to identify your operation's strengths and weaknesses. Be honest!

3 Specifically state your operation's objectives. Do you want to increase customer traffic? Maximize profits on the guests you've already got? Turn once-a-month-guests into once-a-weekers?

4 Use those objectives to come up with long-term and short-term marketing strategies.

5 Develop the actual marketing programs. First conceptualize your programs, then break down steps and tasks.

6 With an outline of tasks required for each program, you'll be able to establish your budgets and back-timed schedules. Begin delegating responsibilities to your staff.

7 Once the program is completed, evaluate your results. Was it a success? Worth the investment? Worth doing again next year?

What Went Wrong?

If you get to number seven and answer "no," here may be some reasons why:

- **Inadequate market research. Did you analyze your research correctly?**
- **Unrealistic goals. Did you take into account the resources of your operation? Be careful not to set goals that are so ambitious they frustrate your staff.**
- **Ineffective promotion. Choosing promo campaigns because *you* find them appealing doesn't guarantee a captive audience. Promotions must evoke a positive customer response.**
- **Poor internal communication. Provide direction, use employee incentives, train, train, train! Keep your people informed. You can't do it without them.**

38 Get the Message?

Designing effective marketing materials

"This is not Burger King. We do not do it your way. This is the county jail. You will do it our way."

— Sign in Chicago's Cook County Jail cafeteria

Well-designed point-of-sale and marketing materials are as important to the success of your operation as well-trained servers. In fact, the two go hand-in-hand. Together they can convince guests to attend your special events, order a new drink or menu item or take advantage of a special-price promotion. Now that you've trained your servers to sell, be sure to give them the most effective sales tools to do the job.

Designing effective marketing and merchandising materials is the subject of thousands of books, videos, and art schools degree programs. But that doesn't mean you have to hire a high-priced graphic design professional the next time you want to print a poster or send out a flyer. There are some basic design principles you can follow to get the most out of your *own* designs.

Whether it be a one-page mail-out brochure, invitation, poster, coupon, table tent, or a flyer, each of your designs has three main objectives: Grab the reader's attention, convey the message and entice the reader to act. If your marketing materials don't achieve all of those goals, you've not only wasted money, time and effort — you've lost a valuable opportunity to reach your customer.

1. Grab the reader's attention. Be dramatic. Use color, bold graphics, photographs or illustrations, and eye-catching typefaces for maximum impact. But don't think you need to use every possible inch of space.

Remember that negative white space or blank space on the page can be a powerful force in drawing the reader's eye into the information.

2. Convey the message. Be sure your copy answers all the following questions that are pertinent to the subject: What is it? When is it? (The event's date or the dates the coupon is valid.) How much does it cost? Who is it for? Everyone? Just members of the Frequent Dining Club? Where will it take place? Are there any special restrictions or qualifications?

3. Entice the reader to act. This is less a function of the marketing piece's design as it is of the offer itself. But if the design fails to highlight a particularly good offer, or makes it difficult for the reader to understand the offer, then the material has failed to relay the full message.

Free For All

When you see an ad, what motivates you the most?

a.) Buy one for $9.99, get the other for one cent.

b.) Buy two, get 50 percent off

c.) Buy one, get one free

Although all three offers are the same, the last one generally pulls 40 percent better. Remember to use it in your marketing materials.

39 A Sure Thing

Stealing marketing/promotion ideas from the competition

"Managing is gettin' paid for home runs that someone else hits."
— Casey Stengel

Restaurant and bar operators are notoriously swamped with work. Who has time to sit around and dream up effective marketing schemes? Most have seen too many of their promotions fail to provide a good enough return on investment to make it worth their while.

But if you want to survive in this business, you have to get people through your doors. Why not let another operation go through the initial trial and error of execution? Once a marketing idea has proven successful for your competition, snatch that idea, improve on it, paint it a different color, tailor it to your operation and – *bingo!* – you're well on your way to a sure thing.

Leave no stone unturned. Don't limit your search to the restaurant industry. Service-oriented businesses of all kinds are thinking up effective marketing schemes. Check out the local retail outlets, grocery stores, hair salons, car lots, Laundromats, even bowling alleys.

A furniture store in Denver ran an outrageously successful Halloween promotion: *Buy your furniture now (the store identified a brief time frame) and if it snows on Halloween, you get it all FREE.* Customers broke out their credit cards like never before – regardless of the sunshine predicted for that day.

The promotion even became a news story covered by local media outlets. There's nothing like a little free publicity to get people through your doors.

Would a spin-off work in your operation? You can decide that for yourself. But keep in mind that the most satisfying ROI is the one that comes after a promotion goes off without a hitch, with little stress and strain required of you.

But just because you've stolen a can't-miss marketing idea – one proven to be successful somewhere else – doesn't mean you're home-free. You'll still have to execute the idea.

To get off on the right foot, define your objective. What are you trying to accomplish? *"I want to raise sales"* is probably too broad. *"I want to raise bar sales during the lunch shift"* brings it into focus, enabling you to identify specific, goal-reaching steps. After all, if you don't know where you're going, how are you going to get there?

Don't Get Out Much?

Enlist the help of your employees to help you come up with new marketing ideas. How many do you employ – 25, 50, perhaps 100? Each one of them probably visits other bars and restaurants three times as often as you and, if motivated, can keep an eye peeled for winning promotions. Consider rewarding or at least recognizing those who bring in the best ideas that you end up implementing in your operation.

40 An Inside Job

Staffing up your marketing efforts

"One of the stepping stones to a world-class operation is to tap into the creative and intellectual power of each and every employee."
— Harold A. Poling, Chairman and CEO, Ford Motor Company

What comes to mind when you think about marketing your restaurant? Perhaps it's the last promotion *you* ran. The customer football pool *you* started. The invitations *you* sent out to build New Year's traffic. *You.* That's who usually thinks up and executes your marketing plans. Or if it isn't you, it's probably a manager under the gun to get people in the door.

The good news is that your get-'em-in-the-door guru need not shoulder the burden alone. Everyone in your operation has a stake in making it successful. After all, don't your servers prefer a full section? Doesn't the tip jar overflow when guests are stacked two-deep at the bar? Doesn't everyone cash in when the place is packed?

It stands to reason that your marketing strategies should include your front-line people. That doesn't mean you should have employees dress up in chicken costumes and wave people in from the street corner out front. It does mean you should have them *join* you in the effort to build traffic. How do you get started? Call a staff meeting and ask what each person can do to generate new and repeat business. Identify specific areas of opportunity. For example:

- *Acquiring new customers*: Establish an incentive for employees to encourage friends and family to come in for cocktails or to dine at your restaurant. For each party brought in, the person responsible gets to put his or her name in a drawing for a prize at the end of the month.

- *Increasing the frequency of customer visits*: How does your staff get guests who come in once a month to come in twice a month? Invite them. Sounds simple, but it's an often-overlooked form of hospitality. Insist that hosts and hostesses thank every departing guest — by name if possible — and always invite them back: *"Come see us again, Mr. and Mrs. Miller!"*
- *Getting first-time customers to come back*: Give your staff the power to pamper first-timers. A pitcher of beer or a complimentary appetizer might be in order. Or samples of house specialties. Or at least a thoughtful overview of the menu and wine list. Take care of new guests and repeat business will take care of itself.

Involving your staff in the marketing process will promote ownership not only in the ideas generated, but also in the well-being of your bar or restaurant. Be sincere in your approach and odds are your employees will be sincere in theirs.

Field of Dreams

If your operation is like most, you've probably got a few college students moonlighting on your waitstaff or in the kitchen. Find out what they're studying. They all have talents beyond their usual job responsibilities — maybe a few can test their school-book knowledge while helping you with your marketing efforts. Have a marketing major help plan your next promotion. Seek the help of a graphic artist to design flyers and advertising for the event. Ask a PR student to work on getting media coverage. Have a music major audition and book bands for live performances. It's cheap, almost-professional marketing help *and* it shows your employees that you respect them.

41 Be My Partner

Get your suppliers involved in your marketing

"Every restaurateur wants the best service, the best quality and the best prices from his vendors. He can pick any two."
— Anonymous restaurateur

Your suppliers know that to successfully push their new products, they need to reach the end customer. And your operation is full of end customers.

That's why you can insist on the help of your suppliers in your marketing efforts. After all, your marketing increases sales of their products. You should not only expect their marketing help, you should aggressively demand it.

It makes good sense for all your suppliers to want to help you increase your business because it's the only way they can increase their own business.

Remember that those customers are your most valuable asset so be careful what kind of supplier hype you subject them to. Be sure that any promotion a supplier suggests for your operation is something your guests will enjoy.

Don't risk alienating longtime guests by allowing a promotion that isn't suited to your typical crowd.

Here are some other aspects you should always insist on:

- New customer traffic. Insist that every promotion brings in new guests to not only try out your operation, but try out their new product. And be sure the supplier is willing to handle all the advertising necessary to bring in those new guests. Your annual marketing budget is a pittance when compared to the millions they put into advertising their products. Why not get a little free publicity for your place? Ask to see all the marketing materials they distribute with your operation's name on them.

- Staff training. Smart suppliers know that the most effective promotions are the ones that make people buy the product again and again. To do that, they need the help of your staff. Here's where your supplier can help you the most. Allow them to come into your next staff meeting to share with your waitstaff product knowledge and upselling tips for the product category in general. Tell them that during the training, they can use specific examples that refer to their product, just as long as the base of the training is in selling more of the overall product category. After all, if your servers and bartenders sell more of the category, they automatically sell more of the suppliers' product.
- Staff to handle everything. Your managers are busy enough already. You don't want them scurrying around trying to manage the event for your suppliers. Insist that they supply the manpower necessary to manage the event.

Who Wins?

Too often, your suppliers and manufacturers forget what promotions are all about. You don't need trinkets, and neither do your guests. You need customer traffic. They need a fun experience at a fair price. Sure, if you offer someone a free T-shift or key chain, they may try a new beer, but next time they come in, they're back to the same old brew – and your operation hasn't gained any new customers. Who benefited? The rep met his quota for the month, but he didn't gain any long-term customers for his product. Poorly conceived promotions help no one.

Mix and Match

Coordinate your marketing materials

Monday morning your radio alarm goes off. An announcer for the corner pub spouts off a spot for a Tuesday two-for-one special. You step outside and pick up the newspaper. There's another ad for the pub's Tuesday special. There's a flyer in your mail, same place, same offer.

"Genius is one percent inspiration and 99 percent perspiration."
— Thomas Edison

Tuesday night comes and you find yourself saying, "Hey, let's stop by the pub for a couple of cold ones." You grab your special customer card and head downtown. The place is packed.

Why'd you go? Was it the radio spot, the newspaper ad, the direct mail piece, the customer discount card, the offer? Yes. And no.

Any of those mediums, handled correctly and with a good offer, would generate *some* response. But all of those elements combined and coordinated with the same message dramatically increase response.

The same can happen to your operation. Whether you're building a marketing strategy for an event or for the whole year, think integration and start planning. Choose the specific market you want to reach and get creative about finding ways to reach them.

For example, if you're hosting a wine and cheese event, start with your database — all your best customers should be listed there by their food and drink preferences.

Then look for local gourmet clubs and wine-tasting groups. Ask for membership lists. Get a charity involved and donate a percentage of your profits for a copy of their mailing list. Post flyers on cars at similar events — or even in your competitors' parking lots!

To add to your marketing mix, look for innovative ways to use mass media. Place an ad in a theater program or the gourmet section of your local paper.

Choose a radio station that reaches your target audience. Whether it be a classical community station or a hard rock college station will depend on the event you've planned.

Then just do it. How? Plan it out — on paper — in advance. Start at the beginning of the year and map out what you want to achieve. Include events, day-to-day marketing strategies and goals you hope to reach that year.

Most important, set deadlines. Because as Duke Ellington once said, "Without a deadline, baby, I wouldn't do nothin'!"

Getting Started

Put it in writing. List all the reasons you want — and need — to advertise.

- **Set specific goals: *"Increase bar revenues by 10 percent." "Sell a minimum of 25 bottles of wine." "Increase happy hour traffic by 12 percent."***
- **Budget. Before the campaign ask yourself *"How much do I have to sell to pay for the campaign? How much to make it successful?"* Look for a 10-to-1 ROI. In other words, for every dollar you spend, you should get $10 back.**
- **Test it. Before you sign a year contract with a newspaper or radio station, test the medium with a campaign.**
- **Measure it. Every marketing technique you employ should be measured so you can make profitable decisions on the next campaign.**

43 Market Your Calendars

Promotions for every occasion of the year

Struggling to come up with a theme for your next bar promotion? Go to your calendar. Each month of the year features several occasions worthy of celebrations.

Just pick the one or two each month that best suit your operation – and get into the spirit for each by planning special offers, contests and themed specialty drinks.

The following list provides a year's worth of holiday and seasonal promotional ideas, along with standard dates if applicable, to mark on your calendars:

January New Year's Day (1st), post-holiday blues, National Pizza Week, Super Bowl.

February Ground Hog Day (1st), Lincoln's Birthday (12th), Valentine's Day (14th), President's Day, Chinese New Year (17th), Washington's Birthday (22nd), Mardi Gras, National Cherry Month.

March St. Patrick's Day (17th), first day of spring.

April April Fool's Day (1st), Easter and Passover, post-income-tax-filing celebration (15th), National Secretaries' Week, Arbor Day.

May May Day (1st), Armed Forces Day, Memorial Day (30th), Mother's Day, Kentucky Derby Day, National Pickle Week, National Tavern Month, Victoria Day (Canada).

June Flag Day (14th), first day of summer, Father's Day.

"If you strive to be one percent better every day, how much better will you be in 100 days?"

— Larry Grieswisch, Co-owner, VP, Jackson's Hole Sports Grills

July Canada Day (1st), Independence Day (4th), Bastille Day (14th).

August Washington State Wine Month, tailgate parties, picnics.

September Labor Day, back to school, Grandparent's Day, first day of autumn.

October Columbus Day (12th), United Nation's Day (24th), National Wine Month, National Restaurant Month, World Series, Halloween (31st).

November Election Day, New York State wine month, Veteran's Day (11th) National Split Pea Soup Week (2nd week), Thanksgiving Day.

December Repeal of Prohibition Celebration (Dec. 5, 1933), Pearl Harbor Day (7th), first day of winter, Christmas Day (25th), Boxing Day (26th).

In the Mood

Get creative with your promotions. For instance, everyone throws a St. Patrick's Day party, but how many celebrate Boxing Day Dec. 26th? One operator decided this was a prime opportunity to boost after-Christmas traffic while educating his guests about holiday traditions around the world. With a little research, he found out that the Boxing Day tradition dates back to feudal times when lords allowed their serfs to take a holiday the day after Christmas. The lords and ladies would bring the serfs gifts of food and clothing. Years later, British workers began spending Boxing Day in their favorite pub tipping pints and eating "bangers and mash." Today, the creative American operator invites his Boxing Day guests to enjoy bangers and mash, yards of ale and traditional British toys at his place.

44 Don't Worry, Be Happy

Presenting a profitable happy hour

"Work is the curse of the drinking classes."
— *Oscar Wilde*

Bar patrons everywhere look forward to sipping a cold one in a lively atmosphere as a wrap-up to their hectic work day. Everyone loves a good happy hour – except, usually, the bar or restaurant operator.

Competition has gotten fierce in the industry as operators have been forced to compete for those happy hour patrons, continually trying to offer a better deal than the operator next door.

Of course you want your place to be "*the* place to be" after work. But as you lower prices to offer unbeatable deals, you have to wonder if the extra traffic makes up for the low margins.

Don't worry. Your happy hour promotions can be as profitable as you want them to be. You'll just need to train your staff to maximize their sales during that happy hour while providing a great experience so guests will want to stick around – or come back during regular hours. The key is to set realistic goals for your happy hour promotions.

Don't just arbitrarily lower prices to beat the competition. Offer specials that provide a server with an easy upsell opportunity. A lot of bar patrons have come to expect two-for-one drink specials. Train servers to attach an appetizer sale to the deal. For example, "*You folks want the two-for-one draft deal? Great! Tonight we're also offering a heaping plate of our Macho Nachos with our two-for-one drafts for just $3.50 more.*"

Or offer regular drafts at "happy hour" price, but offer an upgrade to a large draft for just a dollar more. The same goes for well drinks: "*Would you like to try Bombay in that Gin and Tonic? During happy hour it's just 75 cents more.*"

Run server incentives to provide extra motivation. For example, reward a lotto ticket to the server who's able to upgrade the most well-drink orders to premium brands or regular drafts to larges.

Another effective way to maximize happy hour profits is to convince those guests to stick around for dinner, a game of pool or a big football game. Just train servers to engage customers in casual conversation and invite them to stick around.

Then reinforce your training by offering a five dollar bill to the server who's able to convince the most happy hour patrons to stay for dinner. Just have bar servers count the cocktail-order tabs that they turn over to servers in the dining room.

Timing *Is* Everything

Sure, all good things must come to an end. But why limit your profits when you don't have to? Many restaurant and bar operators still make it a practice to announce a booming "Last call!" at the end of happy hour. Sure, at 1:30 in the morning it's time to clean up and go home so you'll have to call a last call. But why at happy hour when you want those guests to stick around? Also, train your waitstaff the importance of good timing. Teach them to sell heavily around quarter-till so customers will have a fresh one in their hands at the top of the hour instead of beginning to pack up and leave.

Please Be Seated

Games and other activities to keep customers at the bar

"The most expensive thing in a restaurant is an empty chair."
— Cris Roshko, Toronto Restaurateur

It doesn't take a marketing genius to figure out that keeping customers in their seats means higher beverage profits. Today's competition makes it more important than ever. That's why the industry is seeing such a grand-scale emergence of games and activities that keep people at the bar.

Whether it be live bands, sports broadcasts, karaoke or a simple game of shuffle board, restaurant and bar owners everywhere have discovered the importance of increasing customer "seat time" — and more important, maximizing sales while they have the captive audience.

For example, today's pool-hall doesn't conjure up the same sleazy image it once did. Respectable "Old English-style billiard rooms" are a hot concept. And why not? Pool tables provide a prime opportunity to maximize bar sales — when players are shooting well, it's because of the drink. If they're shooting poorly, it's because they need another.

And as the video game generation grows up, the hottest concepts are interactive satellite games like NTN or QB1. "Business was a little slow when we first started using NTN," says one manager, "But now we have a lot of regulars who come in every week just to play. Overall, it's increased seat times an hour and a half and once customers start playing, check averages on a four-top go up at least $20."

But the trick to using these activities to full benefit is to train your waitstaff the importance of good timing. A game of NTN, for example, runs half an hour. Train servers to sell heavily five to 10 minutes before the end of the game. If a player has a full drink, he or she is more likely to stay for the next half-hour game. Each variety of game has it's own duration, but each can be worked effectively for maximizing sales. QBI, for instance, is a four-hour commitment. If servers begin suggesting it about 15 minutes before happy hour ends, you may keep patrons for the entire evening.

The timing principle also applies to live music. Have the band start and be at the peak of their performance at the time guests usually begin to file out. If slow-down typically begins at 10 p.m., have the band start a little after 9 o'clock.

Sports on TV is also very effective for keeping a captive drinking audience and several broadcast companies offer bar operators great multiple-game deals. Careful, though. If your regular crowd is interested only in the "home team," you'll end up paying for games no one's interested in. Just be sure you know your customers.

Beat the Band

Many bar operators have given up hiring live bands because the money generated often fails to exceed the costs of marketing and band "freebies." Why not put more of the responsibility on the band itself? Those up-and-coming acts have much to gain from performing to a packed house. So instead of providing them a set wage, tell them their pay is the door fees and put them in charge of promoting their performance. Give them some guidelines on promoting through posters, fliers, mailers, phone calls, etc. When they promote the show at other gigs, they'll ultimately promote your operation – at no cost to you! Limit the band's guest list to three guests per band member. They won't mind since every paying guest means more cash in their pockets. And instead of providing unlimited drinks for the band, give each performer three drink tickets, redeemable that day only.

46 Join the Club

Frequency clubs

"I wouldn't want to belong to any club that would accept me as a member."
— Groucho Marx

Beer drinker "mug" clubs, wine sampler or connoisseur clubs, tequila shooter clubs — they're all tried-and-true methods for getting your best customers to come back again and again. What any frequency club tries to do is maximize revenues from the guests who visit most often.

But it's not like the guest doesn't get anything out of it: Customers love frequency clubs because of the sense of ownership — the sense of belonging to something. They've proven they like your concept and will come back again and again — as long as they get something out of the relationship, too.

If managed well, those club members are your best marketing source. They provide your operation with constant traffic and word-of-mouth advertising that brings in their friends. So treat them like your most valuable asset.

Most people join because of a special offer. Others join because their friends encourage them. You should never, ever charge a membership fee. The club is a marketing tool for your operation that will generate endless revenues and new traffic. Why should the club member pay? It's important to make joining the club as easy as possible.

And once they're members, your staff is instrumental in making them feel welcome every time they come in. What's the worst crime you can commit against your club members? Not recognizing them when they walk through the door. So train all your front-of-the-house employees to treat members as your operation's most exclusive VIPs.

By the way, that's also the best way to feed your database with personal information on each club member. It's up to your staff to find out what the member does for a living – perhaps his or her company is looking for a Christmas party location. When is the member's birthday or wedding anniversary? Of course you'll offer an invitation to your place to celebrate the occasion!

Can We Talk?

Maintaining constant, personalized communication with club members is an essential part of maintaining your frequency club membership base. And there's nothing more effective for bringing club members back than personalized communication sent to their home. Consider printing a monthly or quarterly newsletter for your club. It doesn't have to be much – maybe just four pages about your operation, information about other club members (birthdays, anniversaries, etc.), menu and drink specials to be featured over the next month. Include a different coupon in each issue, expiring at the end of that month.

47 Just a Taste

Presenting beverage-related special events

Whether it be a wine-and-cheese party, a microbrew-tasting dinner or a margaritas and Mexican food fiesta, beverage-related events are great marketing vehicles for your operation. Not only will you raise beverage profits for the evening, you'll create a perception that your place is the "source" for that particular beverage category. But careful planning is the key. You can't just decide to hold a major party one day and expect to be putting it on in a couple of weeks. Here are some tips on staging your own:

"For us, it may be just another meal. But for our customers, it's always a special occasion."

— Sign in the kitchen of White Fence Farm, Lakewood, Colo.

- Decide what type of event you want. How often will it be held? Elegant black-tie affairs are best held once a year, but casual "tasting" dinners could be pulled off once a month. Will you have expert speakers, presentations and/or entertainment, or will it be less structured?

- Will you sponsor the event alone or ask a beer, wine or liquor company to co-sponsor? You'll find that beverage companies are most willing if their product is the only one featured. But perhaps you'd prefer to highlight a selection from several companies. You may still be able to get a discount on supplies.

- Once sponsors are squared away, decide what beverages to feature. First do a taste test. Then ask your chef to get creative with a menu to complement the selections. It's a good opportunity to showcase your chef's talents, but be careful not to divert too radically from your operation's normal cuisine.

- Since it's a special event, set pricing just a little higher than your operation's average per-person meal with beverages, but not radically out of line with your normal pricing.
- Decide how you will promote the event. Open to anyone? Have on-premise posters printed and hung throughout your operation well in advance. Limited seating for your best customers? Put together a mailing list and have formal invitations printed. Be sure you include an overview of the evening's menu and beverages as well as all the specifics.
- Decide where the event will be held. Can you afford to shut down the operation for a large event? Do you have a party room for a smaller event? Consider holding smaller events in the main dining room during regular business. That way, other guests will say, "*Hey, how do I get invited to the next dinner?*" Be sure servers working the event are well-trained and knowledgeable about all the beverage and menu selections.

Who's the Host?

Someone should be designated as "host" for the evening. Will that person be you? A beverage company sponsor? A local wine maker? The host's duties should include formally greeting guests when they come in and again when they're seated for dinner, giving a brief speech about why your operation is hosting the event, introducing sponsors and special guests and talking about the beverages and menu for the evening. The key is to be brief. Sponsors, who will expect their own turn to speak, should be encouraged to do so, but discouraged from making too blatant a sales pitch.

48 You're Invited

Controlling marketing mailing costs

"Making big bucks in the service business isn't that hard. First learn how to make money faster than you can spend it."
— George Mannion

What's the most effective way to get customers to come back? *Invite* them. No matter how well-designed your on-premise promotional materials, you run the risk that guests won't notice them. But if you write guests a note that simply *invites* them to come in and mail it to their home, you increase your chances of welcoming them back. If used effectively, your database can be your best marketing tool.

Each time you collect a business card, add the guest to your mailing list. Or utilize the tried-and-true "fishbowl" method of collecting guests' business cards. Assign a staff member the duty of entering all the names and cross-referencing records to avoid duplicates. Have your staff help you fill each record with even more useful information on that guest. Who's getting married? Who's having a baby? Who's celebrating a birthday? An anniversary? Keeping correct information in your database can open up all sorts of marketing opportunities. For instance, write a letter to the guests saying, "I noticed you have an anniversary next month. Can we do anything special for the occasion?"

The only problem with database marketing is the high cost of today's postal rates. Follow these tips to keep your mailing costs down:

- By pre-sorting your mailings by zip code, including each mail customer's four-digit code, you can get a discount of about 15 percent on first-class mailings of 500 or more and third-class mailings of 200 or more.

- Join forces with another small company. If your volume is too small to qualify for discounts, you'll split the savings. Look for postal "pre-sort" companies in your area. These time-savers combine mail from several small businesses for pre-sorting and bar coding so all share in the savings. Contact your local Post Office for a free directory of private mailing and pre-sorting services.
- Postcards are a quick, convenient and inexpensive way to get your message across. And you can save 10 cents per piece – even more on bulk rates.
- The U.S. Post Office offers a free service to help you avoid costly mistakes caused by bad addresses. The Diskette Coding Service will update your mailing lists, correcting faulty street names, city names and zip codes. Simply send your address files on PC disk and they will standardize your address records, correct your regular zip codes and add each mail customer's four-digit code, which can save you 20 percent or more on your mailing costs.

It's in the Mail

Use this checklist each time you send marketing materials out in the mail:

- **Does it get your customer's attention?**
- **Does it identify a customer need?**
- **Does it identify how that need can be met?**
- **Does it persuade your customer to buy?**
- **Does it entice your customer to act?**

If you answered no to any of these questions, rewrite your marketing material.

49 Stuck in Traffic?

Satellite bars eliminate long lines at the bar

"Everybody should believe in something. I believe I'll have another drink."
— Wilson Mizner, Los Angeles Restaurateur, 1938

If time really is money, think of the thousands you lose every year by letting your customers wait too long in line for another drink. How many *more* thousands have you lost through customers who have gotten fed up with waiting and gone to the bar next door?

Sure, big crowds are a sign of success — the one thing every operation strives for. But if you can't manage those crowds effectively, keeping people happy with drinks in hand, you'll lose guests quicker than your bartender can say *"Who's next?"*

One solution may be to hire another bartender for back-up during your busiest nights. But if your customer traffic tends to be erratic, you may run the risk of overstaffing bartenders on nights when the crowds just don't turn up.

A better bet is to set up "satellite bars" in other locations within your operation. Instead of standing five-deep at the main bar, customers can head to opposite corners of the building to grab another cold one.

Satellite bars don't have to be fully equipped with the usual bar accouterments and staffed by a knowledgeable bartender. Try setting up simple "mini-bars."

Train one of your cocktail servers to mix a few of your operation's more popular drinks. Or just set out a bucket of your most popular bottled beers on ice. Most servers won't mind this duty during your busiest hours because, chances are, they'll make the same or better tips without having to fight through the crowds. And guests are happier because servers have an easier time getting their drinks to them cold and fast.

Patios are always good locations for permanent satellite bars, but consider other locations. Look at traffic patterns through the operation. Traffic always backs up most around the bar, so find locations directly opposite or in areas that aren't generally as congested.

Going Mobile

When your operation is jam-packed and guests can't reach the bar for another drink, send the bar to them! Have one of your cocktail servers carry around a bottle and some shooter glasses. Plenty of nightclubs out there are doing an astounding business with these mobile drink dispensers. The shots sold are often high-margin items that blend plenty of low-cost mixers with a small amount of alcohol. The best way to sell them is to be creative with your presentation so the drinks catch your guests' attention: Sell "Jell-O shots," use funky shot glasses or glassware, create drama with dry ice. Use your imagination!

50 Suds 'N Sun

Maximizing summer bar profits by prepping your patio

There's something about summer fun in the sun that makes people want to indulge a little more than they might during the winter months. And one of the biggest draws for summer lovers is an operation that provides festive drinking and dining *alfresco*.

"Our best salesperson is an 85-degree sunny day."
— John McQueeney

From May through September, customers love to be outside enjoying hot sun and cool drinks. Is your patio prepped to please? If you have an outdoor dining and drinking area or are considering one, be sure it's the type of place that draws people in and makes them want to stick around.

Here's a patio prep checklist:

- How are your flowers, plants, trees and landscaping holding up to the elements? Do they need a facelift or a simple pruning?
- What is the "sun factor" for any areas affected by direct sunlight? Prepare for those rays with awnings and umbrellas in the right places.
- Do you have an emergency plan to care for your customers during a sudden rain shower? If not, put one in writing and test your staff's knowledge of the plan and its execution.
- If you have a large insect population in your area, consider constructing a screened dining area or installing bug zappers (check state and local health codes).

- Make sure your chairs, tables and utensils are "wind proof." Use napkin rollups to prevent strong winds from carrying away utensils and napkins. Weight down table bases with sandbags or metal weights.
- Are your electrical outlets waterproof? Make sure you have enough waterproof outlets to accommodate your outdoor POS systems, outdoor buffets, chafing dishes and lighting sources.
- Train your employees to use highly absorbent terry cloth towels — not table linen — to wipe up rain puddles or outdoor spills.
- Hire right before the season begins. Train new employees prior to turning them loose on patio or outdoor dining areas.

Five Ways To Sell More Margaritas

- **Use eye-catching glassware and parade them through the patio.**
- **Have your distributor sponsor a tequila/margarita promotion, complete with bright decorations and fun contests.**
- **Test servers' margarita product knowledge — do they know all the ingredients of all your varieties?**
- **Offer "theme" margaritas for holidays. For example, a patriotic red (strawberry), white (coconut) and blue (Curaçao) for the 4th of July.**
- **Pair up premium margaritas with appetizers at a special price.**

Eenie, Meenie, Miney, Moe

Creating a wine list that encourages sales

"The harder it is to read the menu, the higher the prices on it."
— Kelli Rehder

Your wine list is your best sales tool for maximizing wine sales. Where most fail, though, is in their design. The secret to designing an effective wine list is first to know what people look for when selecting a wine, then to know how the customer's eye travels over the menu. Here are a few tips on making the most out of your wine list:

People generally want to know four things about a wine: "Is it red or white?" "Is it sweet or dry?" "Will it go with the entree I want to order?" and "How much does it cost?" And not necessarily in that order.

Most lists are effective if they list the wines by color first, then list from sweetest (at the top) to driest (at the bottom) or vice-versa. It puts less pressure on the customer and it's easier for servers to remember and make suggestions. Indicate this on the menu so your guests know, too. To make your list even more user-friendly, list at least two complementary menu items next to each wine.

Don't list wines by their price. People will inevitably go to the middle of the page for mid-priced wines if they see cheapest at the top, most expensive at the bottom. People don't want to look cheap, but at the same time, they don't want to spend a fortune.

And it's best to offer a wide variety of price ranges. Offered just the choice between a $40 bottle and a $10 bottle, a majority of customers – yes, even in the most chic and expensive restaurants – are going to select the cheaper alternative. If there are no reasonably priced wines, customers are likely to settle for beer or nothing and become rather nervous about what sort of a final bill they're going to receive. But they might have happily paid $20 – you'll never know.

Items listed first will generally sell best. That's quite simply because people were taught to read from top to bottom – and the first item seen is likely to make a stronger impression, while other items have to fight for attention. So list your highest margin wines first or set them off somehow. For the record, items listed second and last will sell better than all the others.

Consider numbering your wine selections so people won't have to attempt pronunciation of *Magyar Állami Pincegazdaság* from Hungary. Just be sure whoever's in charge of the wine cellar puts each wine in its correctly numbered slot, rack or cupboard.

Computer Age Wine Lists

Wine lists don't have to be elaborately designed and leather bound. They could be a simple computer printout generated daily on a word processor. In fact, many smaller operations with lighter wine inventories find that a computer-generated wine list gives them a lot more flexibility. That way, if the Soleo you had on special last night sold out, you can simply call up the file, replace the Soleo with another special or delete it completely, and print it. You'll eliminate the embarrassment of "*Sorry, sir, we've run out of that selection this evening*" and be able to take advantage of your vendor's special offers.

52 Duty Calls

Responsible drinking programs

> **"The innkeeper loves the drunkard, but not for a son-in-law."**
> ***— Jewish proverb***

Each year alcohol-related car accidents account for more than 30,000 deaths, 700,000 injuries and productivity losses totaling more than $50 billion. What are you doing to lower those numbers? Alone, your operation probably can't significantly change the numbers much. But it's in your best interest to try.

Just *one* of those alcohol-related accidents could shut down your operation for good. Some of the possible business-threatening penalties include state-imposed fines, loss or suspension of your liquor license and expensive lawsuits and legal fees.

There are other costs, as well: In an age when people are looking at the bar – rather than the accident site – as the scene of the crime, an alcohol related accident involving your operation is the worst kind of publicity you can imagine. By allowing that guest to drive home intoxicated, you risk losing that customer *plus* all the potential customers out there who'll hear the negative publicity and decide not to patronize your operation.

That's why you have so much to gain from jumping on the "responsible-drinking" bandwagon. It may seem contrary to your operation's best interests: You spend so much time thinking about how to maximize your bar sales, it's hard to switch gears and think about how to most effectively get customers to drink *less*! But you wouldn't be the only operation on the block that's becoming more responsible.

These days, thinking about responsible drinking doesn't just make good sense, it's a good *marketing* measure for your operation.

When you think about it, the marketing value seems painfully obvious: The guy with the keys decides where the group spends the evening. If he knows the "designated driver" can get free non-alcohol beverages all evening long, he may just choose *your* place for that night's destination.

If you offer a free taxi service at the end of the night, guests who have overindulged will finish the evening with you rather than getting behind the wheels of their cars to head to another bar.

You're Outta Here!

Too often, bartenders will keep serving an obviously intoxicated guest because they don't know how to "cut him off" without offending him. For the operator afraid of alienating a good customer, here are some tips on "86ing" effectively:

- **Keep your voice down. Don't cause a scene. Watch your body language.**
- **Be friendly but firm, don't pass judgment.**
- **Once you've refused service to an intoxicated guest, alert all other cocktail servers, bartenders and managers.**
- **If a guest gets belligerent, call a manager or doorman. Usually that's all it will take, but if things get worse, call the police.**

Action Plan

To most effectively put these ideas to work for you, we suggest following these steps:

- Read the book cover to cover.
- Take notes and make a list of the ideas from each chapter that best apply to your operation.
- Give a copy of this book to all of your managers, assistant managers and bar managers.
- Have them take notes and make lists of the ideas from each chapter that best apply to your operation.
- Schedule a meeting to discuss your operation's bar management, staff training and marketing procedures.
- Prioritize the lists of ideas to develop a "Bar Management Strategy," a "Staff Training Strategy" and a "Marketing Strategy."
- Assign a specific staff member to "captain" the implementation of each strategy.

Sample Bar Management Strategy

- Develop procedures for auditing bartenders. Establish policy for managers to act as bar back-up.
- Purchase and install Empty Beer Detector Valves on all keg lines. Double check cooler temperatures, and system pressure.
- Identify one manager as order and inventory manager. Establish routine inventory assessments to control over-purchasing.
- Research and evaluate suppliers based on prices and services offered. Add or delete names on preferred supplier list.
- Establish receiving procedures, designate regular receiving personnel and set delivery times with suppliers.
- Review drink pricing, change menus and drink lists accordingly.
- Evaluate cost efficiency of glassware, napkins, coasters, ash trays, straws, fruit garnishes, etc. Change orders accordingly.
- Research and evaluate cost effectiveness of low- and no-alcohol drink substitutes and mixers.
- Review ice machine service contract and capacity.
- Develop and implement daily pre-shift staff training program incorporating role-play exercises and sales incentives.

Sample Staff Training Strategy

Arrange training schedule, broken down into three categories:

- Customer service
  - Icebreakers
  - Learning and using guests' names
  - ID checking
  - Identifying underage patrons
- Suggestive selling
  - Sales props
  - Descriptive words and phrases
  - Body language
  - Misc. sales techniques
  - Beer, wine, specialty drinks, after-dinner drinks, champagne
- Product knowledge
  - Pouring the perfect draft beer/beer-clean glasses
  - Microbrews and hand-crafted beers
  - Wine and food pairings
  - Wine pronunciation
  - Opening and presenting wine

Sample Marketing Strategy

- Evaluate current marketing methods.
- Research competition, customer needs.
- Set marketing objectives.
- Develop year-long marketing plan.
- Evaluate the design of your wine list, point-of-sale and promotional materials.
- Involve staff and suppliers in marketing efforts.
- Evaluate current happy hour, frequency club and designated driver programs, make changes accordingly.
- Designate staff members to manage customer database, develop database marketing plan.

Pour *More* On!

Pencom International Presents More Ways to Maximize Bar Sales

Show your servers and bartenders how to increase their tips and they'll increase your bar sales. Then do the math. You'll find that a little smart selling adds up to hundreds of additional dollars a day ... up to $25,000 to $100,000 a year, depending on the number of guests you serve daily.

The "How To Sell More..." Series

How To Sell More Wine video

Cheers. When your servers know how to open, serve and recommend wine, you'll double your wine and champagne sales — by the bottle and the glass — and you'll upsell glasses to bottles and house brands to varietals. (TVC-29) $69.

How To Sell More Beer video

Get ahead. Double draft beer sales, move more non-alcohol brews and make up to 25 cents more profit off every beer you sell. (TVC-27) $69.

How To Sell More Premium Spirits video

Frozen assets. Liquidate cocktails into cold hard cash when you upsell well drinks to call drinks seven out of 10 times. (TVC-30) $69.

How To Sell More... posters

Once you've taught your servers to think and act like salespeople, keep their training top-of-mind with these colorful, laminated posters.

10 Ways to Sell More Wine & Champagne (POS-101)

10 Ways to Sell More Beer (POS-103)

10 Ways to Sell More Summer Specialty Drinks (POS-104)

10 Ways to Sell More Margaritas (POS-105)

10 Ways to Sell More Premium Spirits (POS-107)

$7.95 each or all five for $24.95.

Heads Up! Tapping Into Craft Beers video program

More fun than a hoppy Pilsner, the *Heads Up! Tapping Into Craft Beer* video teaches bartenders and servers product knowledge on brewing and serving hand-crafted beers, "Tip Jar" advice on how to sell more craft beers and food-and-brew recommendations (TVC-55) $99. Accompanying Know Your Craft poster features the characteristics of 12 common hand-crafted beers. (POS-209) $7.95 each or five for $24.95.

Johnny Love's Cocktails book

More than 500 off-the-wall drink and shot recipes from San Francisco's best loved bartender, Johnny Metheny, and his popular Broadway Street night spot, Johnny Love's. (PUB-528) $9.95.

Server Dialogue Cards

OK, it's a cheat-sheet. We admit it. These little cards (just 3" x 5") fit inside any order pad to give your servers the smart-selling tips they need – *when* they need them.

10 Ways to Sell More Wine & Champagne (SDC-101)

10 Ways to Sell More Beer (SDC-103)

10 Ways to Sell More Summer Specialty Drinks (SDC-104)

10 Ways to Sell More Margaritas (SDC-105)

10 Ways to Sell More Premium Spirits (SDC-107)

Available in packs of 25 for $9.95.

It's easy. Just **call 1-800-247-8514** to order these products or to receive a **free catalog** of other Pencom International training and marketing solutions. Or fill out and mail in the order form on the next page.

Three easy ways to order

Please clip or photocopy and mail or fax to Pencom International, P.O. Box 1920, Denver, CO 80201 or fax to 1-800-746-2211. For immediate service call us at 1-800-247-8514.

1. ORDERED BY

Print name	Title
Company name	
Address (Please no P.O.Boxes)	This address is: ❑ Home ❑ Business
City	State / Zip
Telephone # (Required to process order)	Fax #

2. SHIP TO *(IF DIFFERENT)*

Print name	Title	
Company name		
Address (Please no P.O.Boxes) ❑ Home ❑ Business		
City	State	Zip
Telephone # (Required)	Fax #	

3. METHOD OF PAYMENT

❑ I've enclosed check # ____________ Payable to Pencom, Inc.

❑ Please charge to the following credit card:

❑ Visa *(13 or 16 digits)* ❑ Discover *(16 digits)*

❑ MasterCard *(16 digits)* ❑ American Express *(15 digits)*

1	2	3	4	5	6	7	8	9	10	11	12	13	14	15	16

Expiration Date

Print Cardholder's Name

4. ORDER

Title	Quantity	Audio	Video	Unit Price	Total

5. SHIPPING AND HANDLING

Continental U.S.

❑ **Standard Two-Day Delivery via Airborne Express**

All orders for in-stock items are shipped within 24 hours after we receive your order. Most orders will be delivered within 2 days of shipment. Add $4.95 for the first item and $1.75 for each additional item.

❑ **Guaranteed Next Business Day Delivery via Airborne Express**

Orders for in-stock items received by noon MST will be shipped that day and delivered the next day. Orders received after 12 noon will be shipped the next day and delivered within 24 hours of shipment. Add $9.95 for the first item and $1.75 for each additional item.

Call For Rates Outside the Continental U.S.

Merchandise total	
Shipping & handling *(see left)*	
Subtotal	
Colorado residents *(add 7.3% sales tax)*	
Grand total